Chick,
This is the one
for the movie

love,
Jim

REACHING
YOUR
SON'S
HEART

REACHING YOUR SON'S HEART

A Heartwarming Story of Healing
for Fathers and Sons

SANDY D. KIRK, PhD

Behold Ministries

Published by Behold Ministries
www.beholdthelamb.org

ISBN Print Book: 978-1-7334-205-6-3
ISBN ebook: 978-7334-205-8-7

Book Designer: Christy Collins, Constellation Book Services

Printed in the United States of America

DEDICATION

This book is dedicated to my wonderful dad who showed me true fatherhood.

It is also dedicated to all the wounded sons and the fathers who long to be restored to them.

I further dedicate this book to all the wise mothers who understand that their sons need a dad, and they choose not to stand in the way.

Contents

He will restore the hearts of the fathers to their children and the hearts of the children to their fathers, so that I will not come and smite the land with a curse.

—MALACHI 4:6

Longing to be Restored to Your Son

The Crisis in America's Young Men

Men of all ages hang on every word. Tom, a fatherless young man, tells what it was like to grow up without a dad. His story seems to break their hearts wide open.

"I can't tell you how much it hurts not to have a dad. My father left when I was three, and as I grew older, I acted out my anger with crime and drugs, just to throw it in his face." The men nodded, looking down.

"My mom tried her best, but she could never be a dad. She couldn't teach me how to throw a ball like a man or build a tree house or fix a car. She couldn't talk to me about manly things, about how to be a real man."

Tom's story touches a raw wound in all of them. They fight to hold back the tears. Some grieve for their own sons, many of whom have built thick walls around their hearts. Some ache for their depressed sons, who may even be suicidal. Others worry about their angry sons, who have expressed their rage with bullying, crime, and violence.

As the men listen, Tom's story splits open their own wound of longing for their sons. But it also tears open their own father-wounds, for no pain on earth crushes a boy more deeply than being abandoned by his father.

Gordon Dalbey, in *Father and Son* writes, "I have discovered that inside every business suit, every pair of faded overalls, every stay-pressed sports shirt, lies the wounded heart of a boy longing for his daddy."[1]

Now the men can no longer hold back. Tom's story is their story. Some cover their faces with their hands. Others simply let go and sob.

When I saw the pain in these dads, I knew I must write this book. I had already completed my Ph.D. Dissertation on this subject at Fuller Seminary. And now for twenty years, at our camp on the gulf coast, we've had hundreds of teens and young adults healed of their father-wounds, many restored to their dads.

This is why I knew I must pass on to fathers—how you and your son can be mended. Indeed, Dads, you are still the most important man in your son's life. Nothing can erase the fact that you are his father.

So let me ask you—do you feel like you've lost your son? Has your depressed or angry boy withdrawn and closed his heart to you? Does he even seem to hate you? Or maybe he is older and long gone from your life.

You may be separated from your son through divorce, through remarriage, the military, or even prison. Every nerve and cell of your being longs to be restored to him, but too much time has passed, and you don't know how to reach him.

Let me encourage you now with a heartwarming story of healing for fathers and sons. Why a book about sons, not daughters too? Primarily because our young men are in such "serious trouble today," as Dr. James Dobson tells us in *Bringing Up Boys*.[2]

Some people ask me, "Is your book religious?" I always say, "No, but it is spiritual because we are dealing with a spiritual problem." In essence, the heart of the issue is an issue of the heart, but only Jesus changes human hearts. And though some would prefer to spend thousands on psychotherapy or psych drugs, what Christ offers you is *free*.

In these pages, you will find five powerful steps for *Reaching Your Son's Heart*. Even if you aren't interested in a spiritual or a heart approach, you can still benefit from these five compelling steps. We will unfold these steps through the power of stories, based on real-life experiences, primarily from sons and fathers at our camp. The story of Bradley and his son Shawn is a composite of these true stories.

This book is actually a parable of what is happening to our own hurting sons in the midst of a massive cultural upheaval in America today. It mirrors the crisis we face with our fathers and sons. At the end of each chapter, I will step in as the narrator, adding current facts and statistics and talking to you as the reader.

Let's go now into the story of Bradley J. Hudson and his son Shawn to find the answers for how to reach your wounded son. We begin with Bradley's pain and shock when he opens his garage door...

PART ONE

The Story of a Father and Son

Climbing the Ladder to Nowhere

When Life Comes to a Sudden Halt

My ambition to climb the corporate ladder came to a screeching halt the day I raised my garage door and found my son hanging from a rope.

My heart dropped to my stomach. My head began to swim. I could barely breathe. I blinked twice, hoping my eyes were deceiving me.

"Oh, God, NO!" I shrieked. I dropped my brief case with papers, once considered vitally important, now flying across the garage floor. But I didn't care. Nothing mattered anymore, but one thing—trying to reach my dying son.

I rushed to his side as he choked and gagged. For a moment our eyes met. In those eyes were bottomless wells of hopelessness. He tried to speak, but he couldn't. Then suddenly his body went limp. He stopped breathing. I was sure he was gone.

I struggled to release his motionless body from the rope, but I couldn't lift his weight and unloose the noose, which dug into his neck. I screamed for my wife.

Then, placing my fingers on his pulse, I gasped. I think I feel a pulsebeat! "Oh God, he's still alive! Please don't let my Son die!" I wasn't a praying man, but I was desperate.

"Shawn," I cried through my tears, "Please don't die! I can't bear to lose you, Son! I've tried to give you a good life. I've given you everything you ever wanted… except…."

I closed my eyes as the thought struck my heart like a thunderbolt: *Could this be my fault?* My heart froze. Then the memories came tumbling in…

And I knew…

The Bond Between a Father and His Son

The Deep Wound of Fatherlessness

It seems like yesterday that my son came into the world. The experience, however, was terrifying. *No, not again!* "Please God, don't take this baby too!"

My blood ran cold as I remembered the birth of our first child. A beautiful little girl—*still born*. My wife had never recovered. Depression had wrapped its tentacles around her like an ugly grey octopus, squeezing the life out of her. She had withdrawn into a shell of grief, and only occasionally could I get close to her.

Now Megan had become pregnant once again, and this time, the pregnancy progressed normally. Even the labor proceeded smoothly, though the doctor had the high-risk team in the delivery room just in case, due to the prior delivery of our stillborn child.

As her obstetrician coached Megan through the delivery, he suddenly stopped mid-sentence and shouted, "Prolapse!"

Instantly, the three team members stepped into action. Our baby—a little boy, whom we had already named Shawn

Michael—began moving down the birth canal, but the umbilical cord had preceded his head. This meant that the blood flow was cut off.

Shawn's heart rate dropped rapidly, and as his head delivered, I could see it was blue and listless. The doctor immediately suctioned his mouth and the rest of his body delivered. But before I could actually see my son, the residents whisked him off to a warming bed. They slipped a breathing tube down his throat and began stimulating his tiny body, trying to coax him to breathe on his own.

My stomach turned over. Megan screamed, "What's wrong? What is happening to my baby?"

I bit my lip to keep from cursing. I could feel the room spinning. *Get a grip, Brad,* I chastised myself, clasping the rail on the bed. *You can't faint!* Somehow, I held myself together, determined to be there for my wife and son.

The doctor and the team gathered around the baby, working feverishly to revive him. I took a deep breath and then did something I never would have expected of myself.

I stepped up, reached out my right hand, and laid it on Shawn's little chest. Through tears of fear and passion, I said as boldly as I could, "Son, this is your father. I am your daddy, and I am telling you to breathe! I command your heart to beat normally!" Then with deep fatherly authority, I cried, "Live, Son, *live!*"

Everyone in the room gasped when they saw the heart rate on the monitor begin to rise. The tiny bursts rose from 50 to 65 to 80 to 120 on the heart monitor. "Pull the breathing tube. Baby breathing on his own," the resident announced.

Shawn let out a loud wailing scream, and everyone breathed a sigh of relief. We all began laughing and crying at the same time.

After blue-printing his feet to the birth certificate, the nurse gently placed our squirming infant across Megan's chest. "Here is your son, already crying for his mama."

Megan held him tenderly and I looked on in absolute wonder. A nurse saw my yearning and she reached down and picked up Shawn. "Time to get these IVs out of mom. Dad would you like to hold your son while we get mom cleaned up and ready to nurse her baby for his first real meal?"

She placed my son—Shawn Michael Hudson—into my trembling hands.

I held him closely and I could almost feel his heart beating against my chest. *This is my son!* I thought proudly. Something within me seemed to bond, like a deep masculine root forming between us—man to man—father to son. It was the greatest experience of my life.

As I held my baby boy, I wondered if my own dad had been there at my birth. I never heard anyone say, but just the thought made me nauseous. I shook my head. *Well, maybe he was a good dad before my mom died, but after that it was sheer hell.*

Megan looked over at me, holding our baby. She smiled and reached for my hand. I felt a great surge of love well up in my heart for this woman who has borne my child.

"Tell me what you are thinking?" she said softly.

"What? Oh, I was just thinking how much I love you and appreciate you for giving me a son."

But she knows me too well, so she pressed a little more. "What else, Brad? You looked so serious and lost in thought."

I hesitated. I never like talking about this stuff. It hurts too much. But this was a moment of rare vulnerability, and my wife, who had just laid herself bare to give me a son, was asking me to be real. *I know I need to open my heart to this woman I love because I have told her so little about my childhood.*

I took a deep breath and sighed. "Oh, Honey, I was just wondering if my own dad had ever felt the way I do about my son's birth?"

"What do you think?" she asked gently.

I shrugged. "No, I feel sure he didn't. If he had, he never would have let my sister and me feel so sad and alone after my mom died. I was only eight and she was seven, but my dad couldn't handle losing his wife. Rather than comforting us in our grief, he went out every night drinking, always bringing in a strange woman to sleep with him. Jenny and I were already in bed but I could hear them laughing and playing around, until they finally disappeared into his bedroom."

"The next morning, they slept in, but Jenny and I had to rummage through a pile of filthy smelly clothes, trying to find something to wear. Then we would forage in the kitchen to find food, but the fridge was always empty, except for beer and maybe some spoiled milk. We usually went to school hungry and stinking and ashamed."

"Oh, Brad!" Megan said sweetly, squeezing my hand. "You never told me. I'm so sorry."

Her compassion caused my eyes to tear up, but I quickly brushed the wetness away, not wanting to appear weak.

I pressed my baby to my chest and drank in the moment. This is my boy, my man-child, my son. I am so proud of him and I will do my best to be a great dad! I am determined never to let him suffer like I did. I vow that I will never be like my dad!

FATHERS AND SONS

Not until many years later would Brad know how monumental this man-to-man bonding is between a boy and his dad. Without this masculine connection, a boy often feels a sense of aching, yearning, emptiness. "The longing to be one with his father is intrinsic to masculinity," writes pastor and best-selling author Gordon Dalbey. Without it, there is a "yawning chasm which the father-wound leaves in his heart."[3]

This bond between father and son is necessary to becoming a secure man. When this longing of a boy becomes crushed or denied, he may venture into manhood with an unexplainable insecurity. This wound of fatherly rejection is called a father-wound.

Author and publisher Stephen Strang, in *Old Man, New Man*, writes, "A father wound cripples a son with the message that he doesn't measure up as a man." Says Strang, "When it comes to a father, silence is crippling, not golden."[4]

That's why it is the intention of this book to lead fathers and sons into healing of their father-wounds. Because I've seen hundreds of young men healed of their father-wounds, I know we can help dads be healed with their sons.

Fathers, I want to tell you again that your son needs you. He may be grown and long gone from your life, but you are still the most important man in his life? You are his father—nothing can ever change that. And whether you know it or not, your son longs for his dad. He may hate you with a passion, but down deep he also yearns for a relationship with you.

Every particle of his being wants to make you proud of him. He hungers to know you believe in him, you care about him and love him. Don't assume he knows it. He does not know it unless you tell him.

FATHERLESSNESS

Tragically, however, every year hundreds of babies are born without a father's signature on the birth certificate.[5] In America 19.7 million kids will go to bed tonight, many crying themselves to sleep because they have no daddy in their home.[6]

In the meantime, look at what has been happening to our young men. Sadly, teenage suicide has tripled,[7] and we have soaring rates of school dropouts, mounting crime and drugs and incarcerations of male millennials.[8]

Bullying has escalated to the point that in 2019, a little boy in Los Angeles received severe brain damage from the violence. And the carnage of mass shootings in schools, by angry boys, has increased to the point that parents fear sending their children to school.[9]

What has happened to our young men? Why are they so angry? Everyone has an opinion: mental illness, easy access to drugs and assault weapons; violent movies, music, and video games. However, none of these are the root cause. None of these deal with the heart. These facts show secondary causes and results, but not the *root*.

Let's see what the facts say. Statistics show that the core of these serious issues with our young men is triggered by one primary cause. The epicenter of the crisis among our boys is one jarring root—*fatherlessness.*

This is a problem of epidemic proportions, and it explains why our broken boys are so depressed and angry. John Smithbaker of Fathers in the Field sums it up: "Boys are broken because they are not being shepherded into manhood" by their dads.[10]

This brings us back to the story of Bradley Hudson and his son Shawn. Brad has made a vow to climb the ladder of success. But there is something deeper and I'm sure you've already seen it. Bradley Hudson is a wounded soul. He carries within him an open sore. It's a painful father-wound, and wounded fathers often wound their sons.

This father-wound in Brad holds him back but it also drives him. It takes a jolting experience to startle him into reality. When he finds his son hanging from a noose, his eyes fly wide open.

Now he continually wrestles with the haunting thought—Is this my fault?

Let's return now to our story, as Bradley Hudson struggles to understand what could have driven his son to such desperation that he would hang himself from a noose...

3

When a Son Closes the Door of His Heart

The Harm of Bottled Up Pain

Megan was a wonderful mother to our newborn baby boy. But I could still see a little hint of sadness in her. I think she still missed her baby girl. Or maybe it was me? I had thrown myself so heavily into my work that I was becoming more and more estranged from my family.

In the evenings, I would slip downstairs to my office, lock the door, flip on the T.V. and sip a few beers to relax, always vowing never to become like my dad with his wild and uncontrolled drinking bouts.

As I progressed up the corporate ladder, I soon had a management position, which brought higher salary but also involved several moves. I didn't realize it at the time, but each time my wife and son had to pull up roots and leave their home and friends, bitterness in the family grew.

Shawn, especially, despised every move. Just when he had made new friends and felt like he had a place where he belonged, I would announce another move.

But I felt like I had to work as hard as I could to provide for my family. I never wanted my son to suffer like I had suffered as a boy.

In high school Shawn was thrilled to make the baseball team, and one morning, he said hopefully, "Hey Dad, I'm pitching today in the game. Can you come? All the other dads will be there."

"Huh? What? You pitching? Uh, okay. Sure," I said absent-mindedly. I couldn't explain it, but every time Shawn mentioned his baseball, I felt a strange twisting in my gut. "I'll try to be there, but I have a big project due tomorrow so I'm not promising."

That night, I came home late. Shawn was waiting for me. As soon as I walked in the door, he tore into me. "How could you?" he yelled. "I was the only guy on the team whose dad wasn't there to support him!"

"Oh Son, I'm really sorry. I just couldn't get away." I sighed heavily. "Please try to understand. I have incredible pressure on me at work. My boss expects me to have this project I've been working on ready by tomorrow. Don't you see that I'm working hard to provide a nice life for you, and I just don't have extra time to go to a baseball game!"

As I turned to walk out of the room, I looked back and said indifferently, "Oh, and by the way, we're moving to the east coast."

Shawn's face flamed bright red and his fists clenched. Cursing, he stomped upstairs, slammed his door shut, and turned up his heavy metal music. I could hear the wild strident sounds coming from his room above my office.

I popped open another beer and drank it way too fast. I fumed, *What does this family expect of me? I work as hard as I can to provide for them, but they don't appreciate anything I do for them. It's never enough.*

I downed a few more beers, getting angrier with every sip. Shawn's music got louder, pounding against the walls. He was obviously trying to unnerve me.

I shouted upstairs, demanding that he turn down his music. He turned it up even louder. Then I lost it.

I don't even remember everything that happened after that because my head stormed with rage. I recall racing up the stairs and beating on his door. He didn't seem to even hear me.

I kept beating and yelling, then body slamming against his door. He must have timed it just right because on my third lunge he opened the door in time for me to fall into his room and crash into his furniture.

I felt a jolt of indescribable pain convulse through my shoulder and right arm. Something about it felt strangely familiar, but I shook it off. I picked myself up, feeling flustered and foolish.

The smirk on Shawn's face as he looked at me, enraged me. I picked up a broken lamp and raised it over my head.

Shawn drew back, and I halted. I saw the look in his eyes, a look of shock and hurt and betrayal. I dropped the lamp and shuddered, *What is wrong with me?*

I hobbled downstairs and slammed the door of my office. I slumped down in my chair, wondering, *Why did I flip out like that? Why was I in such a rage?* I opened another beer and drank until I fell asleep in my chair.

The next morning, I awoke, feeling sick. I groaned as I recalled last night's battle with my son. I stumbled to the bathroom and wretched.

Then I flung myself on my couch and sighed, "Oh, God, what is wrong with me? I am becoming just like my dad!"

When I hit the couch, I groaned in pain. I looked at my arm, now bruised and aching from smashing it against Shawn's furniture. Then I remembered—

I saw myself as a twelve-year-old boy, my sister was eleven. One morning we had searched as usual for food and something to wear to school. There was nothing but some moldy cheese and rotten lunch meat. We went to school in smelly clothes, with hungry bellies. I was so ashamed. And angry.

When we returned home from school, dad was just waking up. He fumbled around the kitchen looking for some coffee. I know this was bad timing, but I couldn't hold back. "Dad, Jenny and I went to school today starving. Can't you ever get some food around here?"

"What!" he yelled. "You little piece of…"

He lunged at me and pushed me into the table and chairs. One of the chairs shattered. He picked up a leg of the chair and started toward me. He swung at my head and I ducked. It knocked him off balance and he stumbled. Now the lion was out of the cage!

I sprinted toward the back door, but he caught me. He picked me up and heaved me off the back porch. I landed on my right arm and shoulder. My bone shattered. I could feel the pain shivering through my whole body. I lay on the ground whimpering in agony.

"You Big Baby!" he sneered. "Suck it up. Can't you be a man, instead of such a girlie wimp!"

That night he locked me out of the house. I moaned all night in the wet grass. Worst of all, he never took me to a doctor, so my arm was ruined. That wrecked all my dreams of ever making it to the Major Leagues with my fastball pitch and my untouchable knuckle ball.

Here on the couch in my office I wondered—*Could this be why my temper has always had such a short fuse? Is this why I always feel a deep ache inside? Is this why my son hates me?*

DEPRESSION AND VIOLENT TEMPERS

Can you see now why Bradley had so much anger buried inside? It is this bottled up grief and anger that often leads to depression or even violence. Boys are taught, "Big boys don't cry." So, their only choice is to stuff the hurt inside, bottle up the feelings, and try to be strong. Dr. Dobson warns that sometimes our wounded boys "cry with bullets."[11] This may result in bullets toward others, or bullets toward one's self.

Gordon Dalbey, in *Sons of the Father*, says, "If a man doesn't deal with his anger, it will deal with him." He explains that the anger either causes him to hurt or "destroy other people, or it turns inward and destroys himself."[12]

What Bradley Hudson didn't realize is that an unhealed father-wound causes an infection deep in the soul. As Dalbey says, "Unattended, this father-son wound can only become infected." That is why, "This breach in the masculine soul, is the gateway for destruction."[13]

Think for a moment about a physical wound. When the wound occurs, if it is not cleansed of all the poison, infection usually sets in. Then it pulses beneath the surface of the skin until finally it erupts in an abscess. Prick the abscess and the poison pours out.

In the same way, the wound of a father can stab the human soul, but if a son stuffs it down and bottles the pain inside, the infection silently grows. Time doesn't heal the wound. Then as an adult, when the pressures of life come, the abscess surfaces. Even the slightest irritation, such as Brad's anger over Shawn's music, can pierce the abscess and cause it to erupt in boiling rage.

Sometimes wives or girlfriends get the brunt of this sudden outburst. Sometimes sons. But more often than not, the root is an unhealed father-wound. That is why deep wounds of fatherlessness must be healed.[14]

A violent temper has destroyed many families, crushed many wives, and broken many sons. But the root is usually the pain of fatherlessness buried down inside. Of course, it can be from other painful causes,[15] but from my experience of working with hundreds and hundreds of teens and young adults, the root is usually a father-wound.

Brad has long buried the gruesome memories of his own father's violence, which he has tried to forget. Holding his feelings inside became his way of coping with grief and hurt. But his father-wound can and must be healed. If not, it will erupt, like a lanced boil, pouring out anger on his son.

That's why I say again, the heart of the problem is a problem of the heart. Hatred, bitterness, resentment, and rage are poisons that simmer inside the sore. The lesion must be exposed to the light, cleansed, and healed. The heart of this problem is a wound of the heart.

From the night of the big fight between Brad and his son, Shawn had pulled away from him and built a massive wall around his heart. But it wasn't the fight that hurt him. It was all the moves to a new town, his dad's lack of support for his baseball, the shame and embarrassment he experienced with his peers, and most of all, it was the rejection he felt from his dad.

His father had remained in the home, yet still was disengaged and too busy to be involved with his life. For Shawn, the deepest wound of all was his father's indifference. Gordon Dalbey says that it is this father-wound that "cuts into the very identity and being of the boy."[16]

Bradley doesn't realize how much his own pent-up anger is affecting his son. Shawn had learned to retreat into the dark cave of his own bedroom. Loneliness had engulfed him, and his music and video games were his way of escape.

Shawn began to imagine how he could take revenge on his father. He visualized himself coming in stone cold drunk, staggering home at 3:00 a.m., disrupting the household, and saying everything he ever wanted to say to his dad. He knew this would crush him because it would remind him of his own father.

He thought about gobbling down a bottle of pills, or even worse, hanging himself from a noose, his dead body dangling from a rope and his dad finding him. But he wondered—would he even care?

All of these ideas seemed deliciously appealing to his tortured soul. He drifted off to sleep listening to his music. He craved the lyrics in these songs. They fed the hatred that gnawed in his gut like a hungry rabid rat. Dark and violent dreams swirled in his head that night.

When he awoke in the morning, his mind was still plotting how he could get revenge.

Then, he knew...

4

Hanging from a Rope

No Father Should Have to Bury His Son

It was a dreary, overcast morning when I swerved my car back into the driveway. I pushed the button to raise the garage door. I was already late to work but I had left an important report at home. I left the car running and waited impatiently for the garage door to lift. *I could swear I left that door open this morning.*

I raced through the garage, and suddenly halted. I caught my breath. I dropped my briefcase and screamed, "Oh, God, NO!"

Papers flew everywhere, but I didn't care. I was frozen to the spot. I blinked hard, hoping I was hallucinating. But no, this was real. My only son, whom I love more than my own life, hung dangling from a rope.

The ladder had just crashed to the garage floor. I saw the rope wrench my son's neck. His forlorn eyes looked up at me. Our eyes met. *Oh, God, our eyes met!* I saw in those eyes nothing but deep wells of hopelessness.

Before I could reach him, he choked and gagged and then dropped his head. I thought my son was dead. His body jerked and his leg kicked involuntarily, but he was gone.

Like a bad dream, I could barely make my legs move. But I finally reached his side and lifted his legs to relieve the weight of his hanging body.

"Shawn! Shawn!" I cried, but the only response I could see was the spastic jerking of his body.

I reached for his wrist to feel for a pulse. I breathed in a sudden gasp. *I think I feel a pulsebeat! Oh, God, there's still hope!* "Shawn, please don't die!"

I could feel the blood pumping through my veins with electric intensity. My heart throbbed wildly as I yelled for my wife.

Megan opened the kitchen door to the garage. Her eyes widened and her face paled. She screamed hysterically.

"Call 9-1-1, Hurry! Hurry!" I struggled to maintain Shawn's body weight, but I was unable to loosen the rope around his neck. "Megan, hurry! I need your help! Bring a sharp knife!"

In moments she returned to the garage, with knife in hand. "What can I do?" she cried.

"Get that ladder and climb up to cut the rope so I can move him. Hurry, Megan, Hurry!"

Megan cut the rope, crying out the whole time, "Shawn, Shawn, can you hear me? Wake up, Shawn?" Even as she shrieked at our son to wake up, she could see that his lips were blue and his face was grey.

"The ambulance is on its way. Oh, what is taking so long?"

I caught my son in my arms and ran into the house, placing him on the dining table. I removed the noose from his neck, and then racked my brain to recall the CPR training I had learned in a high school gym class.

I placed my mouth over his and gave him several deep breaths, but I felt the air escaping through his nose. *Oh yeah*, I recalled. *Clamp the nose, 5 deep breaths, make sure the chest is rising.* I could hear the sound of the ambulance siren coming around the corner.

Megan rushed to open the door and three paramedics dashed in with armloads of equipment. The youngest didn't look much older than Shawn. One immediately placed a collar on Shawn's neck to stabilize it in case his spine had been injured and the two others slid a board under his back. They worked quickly but methodically as one paramedic quietly asked questions.

"What do you think happened? How soon did you find him? Any evidence that he had taken drugs? Is he on any medications? Any medical conditions—diabetes, heart problems?" Even as the man spoke and listened to my answers, the paramedics were starting an IV, listening to his chest, and checking his pupils.

"Irregular and faint pulse but he's got one. No air movement. Pupils slight reaction to light. Bag him."

The paramedic closest to Shawn's head placed a mask attached to a bag and began pushing oxygen into Shawn's lungs.

The young man turned to me and said, "We are giving him some oxygen and some good deep breaths because he isn't breathing by himself. We will keep breathing for him as we transport your son to the hospital, but we have to move quickly. You can follow in your car."

My eyes were trying to take it all in as Megan sat in the corner, reading a crumpled note she had found on the garage floor. She sat rigid, white and still. Her face looked frozen, dry-eyed, with a pain too intense for tears.

Suddenly the reality of it all struck me. My son couldn't breathe. Was he paralyzed? Had his neck been broken in the fall? Would he have brain damage? Now it hit me like a landslide—*My son is dying!* "Why, Shawn, why?"

And then that tormenting thought struck me again. I pressed my hands against my raging head and cried out, "Was this my fault?"

"YES!" screamed Megan, sparks in her eyes. "Here, Brad, read this!" She handed me the rumpled note, and I began to read.

My mouth went dry and my hand shook so hard I could hardly make out the words:

> *I'm sorry, Mom. I can't take it anymore. I know Dad hates me and doesn't care about anything I do. No one, except maybe you, knows how lonely I feel. But soon it will all be over. This pain that constantly stabs my gut will stop. These raging voices of hatred and revenge will shut up.*
>
> *I left the car running, just to be sure. Already, my eyes sting and my throat burns, so I gotta take the leap. But always remember, I love you, Mom. You've been the best mom ever. You always seemed to understand. Please forgive me for leaving you. And when you see Dad, tell him I came to the end of my rope! LOL!*
>
> *I love you, Shawn*

As I read the note, she hammered on, "He was always trying to get you to notice him. To support what he does. Do you see him now, Brad? Do you see? Oh God, oh God," she screamed.

I did see.

I saw my only child, limp and lifeless, being carried out of my home by strangers. I saw how I had completely flopped as a father. I saw how I was never there for him. I saw how I never supported his ball games. I saw his hatred toward me. I saw what an abject failure I've been as a dad. I saw...I had become *my dad!*

And now I knew the answer to my question. Yes, this *IS* my fault. All my fault! *How could I ever live with this reality?* I buried my face in my hands...

Then suddenly, a memory flashed before me. I remembered the birth of my baby boy, lifeless and unable to breathe. I recalled the rush of strength and fatherly authority I felt when I laid my hand on my newborn baby's chest and commanded him to live.

I raced back now to Shawn's side, as the medics carried him to the ambulance. Grabbing his hand, I cried, "Shawn, I love you! This is your dad! I love you! Shawn, I am sorry, for everything. I'll make it all up to you. Please don't die!"

"God, don't let my son die! Please don't take my son!" Then I reached out and laid my hand on my son's chest. With all the emotion and passion of my heart, I commanded, "Live, Son, live!"

Then I clutched my son's hand. "Wait, wait... his hand moved, he just moved!"

The paramedic bagging Shawn saw a flinching of the muscles in his chest. "He's gasping, he's breathing. I'm switching to a partial re-breathing mask. Shawn, take some deep breaths but don't try to move. We're taking you to the hospital. Your mom and dad will be coming right behind us."

With that, the ambulance sped off, siren blaring and lights flashing. I laid my head on Megan's shoulder and wept, "Oh, my God, what have I done?"

WHAT CAN A FATHER DO?

Brad never wanted to hurt his son. No father does. He had bonded with him so deeply when he was born. He had vowed never to wound his son as his own father had wounded him. However, out of his own pain, he had inadvertently made his son feel rejected. Though remaining in the home, his son was basically fatherless.

Brad had driven himself so hard at work that he never realized what had been happening with our teenagers today. He had no idea about the rampant suicides that had been breaking out in this young generation.

When he was young, no one talked about killing themselves, but a 2017 "Pain in the Nation" report said that teenage deaths from suicide rose 84% in the last decade.[17]

According to Dr. Tim Clinton, every day 5,240 teens attempt suicide in America. *Everyday!* That's over two million attempted suicides per year.[18] Today suicide rates have spiked to the point that a study showed one in every ten teens has made a suicide plan.[19]

Dr. James Dobson, a trusted parental authority, said, "The weakening of the family and the absence of caring fathers are the primary reasons why boys are in trouble today." He also cites a report in *USA Today*, showing that teenage boys under fifteen are five times more likely to kill themselves as girls.[20]

I mention these statistics simply to say once more—we have a crisis of depression and suicide in a young generation. Is this the result of father-wounds? Sadly, for the most part—*yes*. Studies show that 63% of all suicides among youth are from *fatherless* kids. [21]

But please understand, my intention is not to condemn fathers. As I've said, it's futile to cast blame. We need *solutions*, not accusations. However, if we know the primary cause, we can now face it and try to fix it. We must face the father-wounds in our sons and help them heal. Fatherlessness is the heart of the issue, and father-wounds are an issue of the heart.

What then can fathers do to slow the onslaught of suicides in our young men? There is an answer, but it will take twelve more chapters in this book to unpack.

We will be looking at the five steps for how to be restored to your son in Section II, but first, we needed to consider the problem. Please remember that this one story of Brad and his son Shawn is based on true stories from hundreds of young people at our camp.

Our approach will be both spiritual and factual. The pain in a son's life didn't happen overnight, but what I'm asking of you is to step into Bradley Hudson's shoes. Discover what he did to restore his relationship with his son and turn everything around.

But first, let me ask you—would you be willing to do whatever it takes to reach your wounded son?

Bradley Hudson decided he must do anything and everything possible to save his boy. Finding his son hanging from a rope jolted him awake. He knew he must slow down, prioritize his family, and spend more time with his son.

He didn't know how or where to begin, but he was determined to do whatever it takes to save him. He couldn't bear the thought of having to bury his boy.

5

Angry Boys Shoot Bullets

Helping Sons Deal with Rage

When Shawn returned home from the hospital, he wanted nothing to do with me. He began slipping out almost every night with his best friend Jamal. He would come in late, smelling of alcohol or weed or stoned on whatever drugs he could find. He didn't care.

It hurt me so badly to see him like this. I tried desperately to reach him, but I couldn't crack through the shell. If I ever saw him, he would brush right past me, bound up the stairs, and slam his door. The message Shawn gave me was, "It's too late, Dad. Leave me alone! I hate you and I always will!"

I felt helpless, but I was determined to reach my boy. What could I do? Take away the car keys? Ground my eighteen-year-old? I knew this wouldn't work.

I immersed myself in psychology magazines, reports and documentaries on teen suicide, and self-help books. I watched videos about recovery programs and medical cures for depression. I found other causes for depression and suicide, but the one common denominator was *fatherlessness*.

I read an article by Emilie Kao, director of the Richard and Helen DeVos Center, entitled, "The Crisis of Fatherless Shooters." She said, "If we are going to prevent the next Parkland (school shooting in Florida), we need to take seriously the need all our young boys and men have for a dad."[22]

"*I know. I get it!*" I thought, smashing my fist on my desk. *I see the problem but how the hell do I fix it? I can't break through to him. Surely there must be an answer!*

Megan handled it differently. A neighbor invited her to church. At first, she hesitated because she felt she would be judged. Surely everyone knew about her son's attempted suicide.

She joined a women's support group in the church, and when she came home, she wanted to tell me all about it.

"Brad these women all have their own heartaches. Some are divorced; some have cheating spouses; some have troubled kids, and some are caring for aging parents. We all need each other's support."

One night she told me, "I decided to be vulnerable today and lay my heart bare. Not only did they surround me with love and support, but they prayed for me and for our son."

I noticed that she seemed happier than I had ever seen her. But silently I vowed, *She won't get me to that house of hypocrisy.* I had long ago concluded—there is no God.

Deep down inside, I was bitterly angry with God. *If He were real,* I thought, *He wouldn't have allowed my mother to die, my childhood to be so lonely, and He wouldn't have given me such a violent alcoholic Dad.*

Furthermore, if God were real, He wouldn't have taken my baby girl at birth. He wouldn't have caused my son to hate me when all I've ever done is work hard to provide for him.

Sometimes Megan would ask me to come with her to church. Angrily I would retort, "I want nothing to do with your so-called God!"[23]

THE SHOOTING

All this time the rage in Shawn's heart kept building to the point that it sometimes seemed he would explode.

He was nearing the end of his senior year, and he refused any guidance from Megan and me. He fed himself constantly on videos and heavy metal music with brutal themes. When he did come home at night, he fell asleep watching sexually sadistic or occult movies. Megan noticed his face seemed darker and he never looked us in the eyes anymore.

One day he accidentally left his phone at home. Megan had seen his password scribbled on a piece of paper when she was emptying the trash from his room. She saved it, and when she tried it on his phone, pornographic sex scenes opened before her eyes.

She scrolled through his pictures, videos, and posts on Instagram. She saw messages to Jamal, showing videos with violent sex, swastikas, pentagrams, and brutal scenes of butchery.

Megan knew Jamal's dad was in prison, and he too, being fatherless, was filled with bitterness and rage. He responded to Shawn with vicious scenes of mayhem, street-fighting, and carnage.

Her heart leapt to her throat when she saw rants about how Shawn and Jamal wanted to blow up the school, kill their teachers, obliterate the frats, jocks, and cheerleaders.

Shawn boasted, "Since I failed to do the job in my first suicide attempt, this time I'll go out in a blaze of glory!"

In a panic she called me. Through chokes and sobs she told me what she had seen. I dropped everything and raced toward home. On the way, I turned on the radio and my heart froze. Blaring from the radio, came the breaking news: "Active shooter at local high school!"

I threw on my brakes and headed toward the school. I arrived in time to see police with flashing lights surrounding the school. Other parents were arriving. The police had cordoned off an area where students ran single file out of the school, searching for their parents.

The cops had dashed into the school, straight into harm's way. More shots rang from inside. People in the school screamed.

I stood watching as young people fell into their parent's arms, sobbing wildly. I could scarcely breathe. I broke into a cold sweat and my body quivered from head to foot. My brain swirled and I was almost delirious with shock and fear.

I tried to listen to the kids as they frantically described the carnage they had witnessed. They were traumatized as they tried to tell their stories. I heard a girl saying, "The killer was a guy in my class. I think his name is. . ."

Just then I looked up and saw Shawn limping toward me. His shirt was splattered with blood and his leg had been grazed by a bullet. He panted, "Oh, Dad, it was horrible!"

I managed to gasp, "Son... are you okay?"

"Yes, but... what I saw was..." He couldn't speak. He sank into my arms, weeping almost uncontrollably.

I wept with him because I was so relieved that he wasn't the killer. I held him tightly, savoring the moment, for this was the first time I had held my boy in years.

By now, Megan had arrived at the school. She too feared that Shawn was the killer, but when she saw him trembling in my arms, she breathed a sigh of relief.

"Who did this?" I asked.

"Some crazy kid," Shawn groaned, "but now he's dead. I saw the police take him down."

As parents and kids began to disperse, Megan and I accompanied Shawn to the emergency room to have his bullet wound treated. At home, we learned more about the shooting from news reports.

School was closed for several weeks as students attended funerals and the school was purged of all remnants of the massacre. When the doors finally opened, the students seemed apprehensive about returning to school.

A solemn hush settled through the hallways where teachers and students had been wounded or killed. Friends could be seen, huddling in small groups and weeping in each other's arms. Kids broke down and cried in the middle of class.

Nothing anyone could say would ease the grief that consumed them. It was like they had been in the midst of a warzone with no protection. Teenagers were traumatized by what they had seen. No child should ever have to witness such a bloodbath. They should never have to experience such horror. Many of them have never recovered.

THE MAIN CAUSE OF SCHOOL SHOOTINGS

When a school shooting occurs, usually catching everyone off guard, communities are devastated and the whole nation shakes.

People raise their voices, attributing it to bloodshed in movies, video games and violent heavy metal music. They point their fingers at politicians and decry easy access to guns. They blame it on mental illness or dangerous drugs. They accuse men of toxic masculinity which, they say, encourages boys to bully weaker students.

Again, however, these are all secondary causes. They are not the root of the problem, for the heart of the problem is a problem of the heart. The facts prove that the primary problem is *fatherlessness*.

Dr. Peter Langman, an expert on school shootings wrote that in one sample study of 56 school shooters, 82% grew up in dysfunctional families without both parents.[24] Did you get that staggering statistic?—**82%!**

Emilie Kao reports, "There is a sobering theme repeated over and over in the biographies of school shooters—the fatherlessness of a broken or never formed family."[25]

Marriage scholar Suzanne Venker found "a direct correlation between boys who grow up with absent fathers and boys who drop out of school, who drink, who do drugs, who become delinquent, and who wind up in prison. And *who kill their classmate(s)*."[26]

HOW DAD'S CAN HELP ANGRY SONS

Coach Joe Ehrmann, an All-American football player and coach, tells us that "Violence is unprocessed grief." He adds, "Boys who can't cry shoot bullets."[27] A case in point is Anthony Simms, known as the Oakland killer, who wrote in his last Facebook post: "I wish I had a father."[28]

Do you see why we must find how to help our sons process grief and anger? Grief is the underlying cause of most depression and anger. Not all, but most.

But in a way, that is really good news, because now you can see how you can be the one who reaches out and warmly helps your son process his feelings.

Yes, Dads, you hold the key to healing the heart of your son. If you can restore your relationship with your depressed or angry son, it will be one more step toward eliminating the crisis with America's young men.

Again, we aren't pointing the finger and blaming you. We are encouraging you to step into your highest calling and help heal and restore your son.

Just imagine—if men everywhere would rise to their calling as a father, we would begin to see a decrease in the rate of suicide and depression and school shootings and bullying and so much more. That's why we aren't knocking or condemning fathers.

We are cheering you on!

So think of ways you can spend more time together, like fishing, throwing a baseball or football, shooting hoops, or building, gardening, landscaping, changing a tire, fixing a car engine. Try to teach him in a language he will understand, but whatever you know how to do, take the time to show him.

If he loses a game or doesn't make something he really hoped for, get him to talk about his feelings. This is how he can process his grief before it becomes huge. He may even need to cry on your shoulder. Then talk about how you can work with him to help him do better. Give him hope.

You say, no that's what mothers do, not dads. My mother would never have discussed these things with me, but my dad did, and he went down in my book as the greatest dad in the world.

TALK TO HIM ABOUT SEX

There's something else you need to talk about with your son, sooner rather than later. You say—no I'll let his mother do that? Why? You're his dad. You understand these things from a man's point of view. I know it can be difficult, especially if you only know how to use crude language. If that's the case, then read up on the subject so you can discuss it in a mature but meaningful way.

I urge you to talk to him about pornography. Did you know that this is how most kids are getting their sex education today? This is very serious because of the violence and abusive sex that is part of the pornographic scene.

Some are calling this "the new drug." According to *The Huffington Post*, every month, porn sites receive more regular traffic than Amazon, Twitter, and Netflix all combined. In fact, 30% of all data conveyed across the Internet is pornography. [29]

Neurosurgeon Dr. Don Hilton warns that the sexuality of youth today has been "hijacked." He points out that because so much pornography involves aggression, this affects the way young people view sex. Hilton says that this addiction can actually "re-wire the brains of adolescents." [30]

We have to face it. Pornography addiction is not harmless. It destroys marriages and distorts marital sex. James Dobson questions, "How did they get that way?"

By exposure to graphic materials that set them aflame. This pattern is responsible for numbers of divorces and dysfunctional marriages. I know this is true because I hear almost every day from women whose husbands are heavily involved with pornography.[31]

Through the years, I've heard many young men burn with anger because their dads never talked to them about their sexuality, about pornography, about how to treat a woman.

But I promise you this—if you will talk to him, he will love and respect you for it. If you avoid the subject because of immature embarrassment, he will probably later resent you for it.

Now let's return to our story and see something amazing that happened to Shawn. No one can tell his story like Shawn himself, so let's listen now to him.

6

"Dad, Where Are You?"

Hear the Cry of a Fatherless Son

Ever since the tragedy at my school, I felt unusually subdued. Jamal and I rarely went out drinking or toking weed anymore. Twice now I had stared death in the face, and it made me think about the future life, if there is one.

Something else had happened at school that I had not told my parents. After school opened, the Christian club asked a young evangelist to speak to the club. They invited anyone who wanted to come, and 500 of us crowded into the gym. I went out of sheer curiosity.

Joshua Kelly, a twenty-two-year-old evangelist had only fifteen minutes to get his message out, but he preached with a passion and sincerity like I had never heard in my life.

To the students in the gym he cried, "How can you stop drugs? How can you stop all the suicides and shootings that are happening in our schools? The answer is Jesus!"

A collective gasp filled the air. What? This guy had the audacity to break political correctness and speak the name of *Jesus?* Didn't he know how uncool this is?

Joshua continued: "You can have all the programs you want, all the activities you want, but there is only One Person who can change the youth of America!"

"Think about it," he said, "If your life were to end thirty minutes from now, where would you go? You cannot go to heaven just by doing good deeds. Jesus said there is only one way: 'I am the way. I am the truth. I am the life.' You must have Jesus!"

My pulse raced. I had never actually heard that Jesus is the only way to God. I always thought that if I was good enough, I could probably make it into heaven. But I had never heard any genuine gospel preaching. Now my heart began to beat faster.

What is this I am feeling?

The passionate young man then invited students to get out of their seats and come forward if they wanted to receive Christ and give their lives to God.

Suddenly, they came. Over 250 high school kids stepped down from the bleachers and filled the gym floor.[32] Jamal was one of the first to go. He grabbed my arm and said, "C'mon, Dude! We need this."

Jerking my arm loose, I cried, "*No!*" Everything in me longed to go with him, but I kept hearing my dad's voice mocking me—"You gullible wimp! How could you fall for that religious stuff?"

At school, most of the kids who went forward to receive Christ, in spite of the recent tragedy, seemed happy. Something was different about them, especially my buddy, Jamal. It was like he became a new man. He no longer wanted to go out and drink or talk about killing people. He was full of love and purpose.

His dad was in prison, so he too was deeply wounded by his father. But now, he kept talking about forgiving him.

After that, I felt hopeless. My one opportunity to find a new life in Christ had passed me by. I felt more confused and broken than ever.

HOW SCHOOLS CAN PREVENT SHOOTINGS

Before we continue, I want to comment on the story above, which took place in a public school 20 minutes from our camp, with one of our former students as the young preacher. This actually took place on May 18, 2018. On the very same day, something tragic happened in a public school in Texas. The irony is stunning.

On that same warm spring day, May 18, 2018, a young man walked into a high school in Santa Fe, Texas. He lifted up, not the gospel, but an assault weapon and slaughtered two teachers, eight students, and left thirteen wounded and bleeding in the hallway.[33]

In the first school in Alabama, students went home full of God's love. In the Texas school, over a thousand students went home—*traumatized!*[34]

According to the *Washington Post*, "More than 236,000 students have experienced gun violence at school since Columbine."[35] This is unthinkable! Many of these kids still have PTSD today. This has to stop!

Contrasting these two events, both on May 18, 2018—the salvation of 250 students in the Alabama school and the slaughter of 10 students and teachers, and the wounding of 13 more in the Texas school—the answer becomes obvious.

Those of us who are older, remember when students respected teachers and wouldn't even dream of shooting up their school. What was so different? Do you recall how prayer and Bible readings and the Pledge of Allegiance were common place. These were spoken *everyday* in public schools. Even when I taught high school during the hippie movement, I was completely free to bring Christ into my classroom.

This is not a political issue. It is a life and death issue. How many of our children have to die before we realize that our First Amendment Right—Freedom of Religion—must be returned to our schools? We need to bring high moral standards back into our schools today.

SHAWN CONTINUES HIS STORY

A few days later, Jamal asked me to go with him to his youth group at church. That night I came home from church with a book. The youth pastor had preached from it and handed one out to all the kids. The name of the book was *Dad, Where Are You?*[36]

At home, with my door locked and a song, which Jamal had recommended, playing loudly, I felt drawn to open the book. The first chapter seemed to drill right into my soul, unearthing my deepest feelings. I couldn't put it down. I read:

"Pouring silently from the soul of a fatherless generation comes a moan of hopelessness. It's an unparalleled cry of pain...." *That's me for sure,* I thought.

"Wailing up from the depths of wounded young men and women, comes the cry, "*Dad, Where Are You?* Why have you forsaken me?"

Wow, that's exactly how I feel. I sighed and laid back on my pillow. Beads of sweat formed on my forehead and dripped down my neck as I read.

The words pierced me. I felt like my soul was being exposed. Then the author wrote, "So pause for a moment to feel inside your heart. Do you feel an ache within? Is there a dull throb pounding somewhere way down deep? Are you afraid to cry for fear the tears will never stop?"

"Maybe you've tried to drown the pain with drugs or alcohol or sex, but when you awaken in the morning you still feel the familiar ache, almost like an old friend. Or maybe your heart has finally numbed, drained of any feelings at all."[37]

I kept reading. It was a short book, but it struck a sensitive nerve. It called me to lift the eyes of my heart to a hill outside Jerusalem. It invited me to look up at God's Son, dangling from two strips of wood, bleeding and dying for me. It drew me to focus on the only Person who will never forsake me or leave me alone.

SEEING JESUS

Now it was like I could see Him, "stripped before the eyes of the world." I could, as the book says, "gaze upon His wounds, His tears, His blood, His pain until you know how much He loves you."[38]

Suddenly, Jamal's song broke through to me. The words seemed to open my eyes and helped me respond to what I was reading:

I can only imagine what it will be like

When I walk by Your side

I can only imagine what my eyes will see

When Your face is before me.[39]

In that moment, I did what the song led me to do and what

the book described to me. I imagined the face of Jesus before me. I looked up at Him with the eyes of my heart. And when I did, I could feel the hardness inside me melting away.

I started to cry, softly at first. In seeing Him, I knew something was happening to my stored-up pain. It was like a great boulder of grief started rolling out of the tomb of my soul. I never knew I had buried so much hurt inside. I could literally feel my heart changing.

Then I read something in the book that seemed to answer all my questions about God. It was a call to look into the Father's cup, which Jesus engulfed on the cross.

I could feel my heart beating faster. A gentle heat seemed to rest on my face, drawing me to read more. I thought I knew all about the cross, but I never knew about the Father's cup. I read on.

"As a blazing inferno mounts and swells then sweeps through a forest, burning down everything in its path, the fire of God's holy wrath against sin has mounted over Jesus."

"Here He hangs, the Man whose only fault is love…. Now the wave breaks. It bursts down upon Him. Wave after wave of the Judgment of God roars down upon the innocent Son… It is not a visible fire, but a spiritual blaze, burning up all your sin in Him."

"The Bible says, 'He was 'stricken and afflicted by God….pierced for our iniquities….The PUNISHMENT that brought us peace was upon Him' (Is. 53:4-5). Yes, Jesus is being punished for you."[40]

To think that God's only Son was punished in my place changed my whole view of God. I realized that Jesus took my hell so I could have His heaven.

Then, I came to the part where Jesus cried with all the passion of His heart, *"My God, My God, why have You forsaken Me?"* (Mark 15:34).

His cry blew my soul wide open. I could feel a trembling somewhere deep down inside. I knew then that Jesus cried the cry of a fatherless son. He wept my cry of abandonment. He was deserted by His Father just like me. He was forsaken by God so that I would never be forsaken by my God.

My heart was thundering now. I felt like I did at school when the young evangelist called us up to receive Christ. I could hardly believe it. He was giving me another chance. There must still be hope.

I fell to my knees by my bed and cried out to Jesus. "Lord, I give You my life. As broken as I am, please take my shattered life. I'm sorry I've resisted You so long, but I just didn't understand. Now I'm blown away by what You've done for me. With all my heart, I give my whole life to You."

Still on my knees, I laid my face down on my bed and quietly cried. I cried for all the ways I've hurt Him with my drinking and drugs and rebellion, and even my attempt to kill myself.

But when I realized how much He loves me and that He was punished in my place and He cried my cry of forsakenness, my sobbing got louder.

I turned up the song, hoping my parents couldn't hear me, but honestly, I really didn't care. I had found the Father I had always longed for, just as He promises: He is "a father of the fatherless" (Psalm 68:5).

At last I knew that I will never be abandoned by my heavenly Father, for He had answered the cry of my heart.

MEGAN AND BRAD RESPOND

Megan heard him and ran down to beat on the door of my office. "Something is wrong with Shawn. He's crying really hard. I'm afraid he's suicidal again!"

I tore up the stairs and paused at Shawn's door. I could hear the intermittent sobs. I started to break through the door.

"Wait… *Shhhh*…" Megan whispered.

"Listen, can you hear that music? He's not playing that raucous heavy metal… Can you hear the words to that song, 'I Can Only Imagine…'"

They both put their ears against the door and listened:

Surrounded by Your glory, what will my heart feel?

Will I dance for You Jesus or in awe of You be still?

When I stand in Your presence, to my knees will I fall? Will I sing Hallelujah; will I be able to speak at all? I can only imagine…[41]

"That's a Christian song, Brad! Something is going on with our son."

I took a deep breath and leaned against the wall. *I have never thought what it would be like to someday stand in the presence of God, like this song said.*

I shook it off, and we both tiptoed away, not wanting to disturb whatever could be happening.

The next morning, Shawn bolted into the kitchen, smiling broadly, carrying the little book.

"Mom, I gotta tell you something. I read the book the youth pastor gave me." Tears sparkled in his eyes. "Mom, I didn't know… I just didn't know…"

He kept shaking his head as though he was amazed at this new revelation.

I sat at the breakfast table, quietly taking it in.

"What? What didn't you know?" asked Megan.

"I thought I knew all about the cross, but I didn't know that Jesus, God's only Son, carried all my anger and hatred and drugs and sex and drunkenness—to the cross. Then He opened wide and drank down every drop of the Father's cup—*in my place*. He was punished for me. Oh, I can't get over it," he cried, shaking his head.

"Jesus Christ drank God's cup of punishment so that I could be set free. He took my hell so I could have His heaven. He took my penalty so I could be forgiven. He cried my cry of abandonment so I would never again be abandoned."

"When I saw what He really did, I realized how much He loves me. I always thought He must hate me for all the terrible things I've done. But no, He already paid the price because *He loves me!*"

"Oh, Mom, can you believe it? I asked Jesus to forgive me and cleanse me and come into my heart. I gave Him my whole life, and now everything has changed. It's crazy!"

Shawn took a deep breath and said, "Now I understand it's not about what *I can do* to deserve heaven; it's about what *He already did* on the cross when He drank the Father's cup. This is the gospel, but I had never heard it."

"I was a lonely boy hanging from a noose, now I'm overjoyed just to be alive in Christ," he gushed happily, hugging his mom and twirling her around the kitchen.

"Hmmm," I muttered skeptically. "Let's see how long this will last."

Shawn turned and looked at me. Ignoring my skepticism, he looked me in the eyes. He handed the book to me and said, "Here, this book changed my life. I want you to have it. You need to read it."

I looked at the book and swallowed hard. The title read— *Dad, Where Are You?* "But this book looks like it's for someone young, not me." I said curiously.

"Dad, look at the subtitle—*The Cry of the Fatherless*. It's for those who were fatherless. Did you ever cry for a real father?"

My heart stood still.

"You *need* to read it. You have a deep father-wound."

Now, as we step into the next chapter, Bradley will begin to discover the seriousness of his father-wound. This will prepare him to take the first of five steps for being restored with his son.

A Father Faces His Own Father-Wound

When Wounded Dads Wound Sons

That evening I locked myself in my office as usual. But this time, instead of turning on the TV, I picked up the little book, *Dad, Where Are You?*

I opened to Chapter Two and my heart sank. It started with a story of a father whose son had committed suicide. This was the last thing I wanted to think about. I opened a beer and read:

A father drifts off to sleep one night when he hears his son Jeffrey slam his bedroom door. At the moment, the sound of his son opening the breach on his shotgun and sliding a shell into the chamber, doesn't register. But the sound of the breach closing sends the father into a panic.

He feels the blood rushing to his feet, leaving his brain empty. Before the full realization dawns on him, he hears the explosion. The sound still haunts him, causing him to awaken at night in a cold sweat.

His four-year-old arrives there first. Seconds later he races into the room, which is splattered with blood. Jeffrey's heart is blown out. Horrified, he grabs his son.

Then Jeffrey, in the throes of dying, looks up with hopeless eyes and says, "I'm so sorry. I'm so sorry."

As this anguished dad holds his dying son, he clings to him and cries, "Jeffrey, I love you! I love you!"

Later he realizes, this was the first time in his life he ever told his son he loved him. He didn't have time to get involved in the things Jeffrey wanted to do. He was too busy making money. Never did he realize the hopelessness and pain that ached in the heart of his son. He holds him closely now as Jeffrey slumps in his arms and dies.[42]

Oh, God, that's what I've done, I thought. *I've been too busy making money to make time for my son's baseball games or things that were important to him. We never had fun together. I don't think I've ever told him I loved him. I just thought he would know it.*

Though it hurt me to face the mistakes I had made, I forced myself to keep reading. "In this true story the father's memory of his son dying in his arms still plagues him. He remembers laying his son's body on the bed and looking at his own hands, covered with blood. 'Oh, Jesus,' he cried, 'his blood is on my hands!'"[43]

The book went on to explain that in a sense, our whole adult generation could say the same thing. "We have blood on our hands. So many broken homes, scattered families, wounded spirits, abused children, aborted babies, lonely teenagers, and depressed young adults."[44]

I gritted my teeth and threw the book at the wall, cursing. "How in the hell can it help me to be reminded of what a rotten dad I've been?"

But I knew for my son's sake, I must press through my feelings and keep reading.

> "Yes, a deep hole has been sliced in the soul of a young generation. Because so many dads were gone from home, driven by work or driven out by alcohol or other addictions, many of you feel like you never really had a dad."

Well, at least I can say I've stayed married to my son's mom. I've provided for my family, and my son has never experienced the shame of wearing filthy, rotten clothes to school, like me.

He never had to come home alone with a little sister, to an empty house, and be mocked as a latch-key kid, like I was. He never got slapped in the face if he dared to complain or shed a tear.

I picked up the book and read a bit more: "Yes, never in history have we seen such a broken, suicidal, hopeless generation. That's why this has been called 'a fatherless generation.'"

I laid the book down and leaned back in my chair. *With all the broken homes, I guess this really is a fatherless generation, but I was fatherless too. My dad was never home, or if he was, he was usually drunk. I'm beginning to see that this is why I've been such a miserable failure as a dad? This is why I have such a volatile temper.*

Wait a minute. This story is beginning to sound like my story. I guess this is why Shawn wanted me to read it?

I tightened my jaw and squeezed my eyes shut. It felt like my heart was ready to burst with emotion. *What's going on with me? I'm tough. I never cry. I'm the strong guy.*

I could feel the pain pulsing inside. It felt like an old scab had been ripped off and the ugly wound exposed. I recalled the words from the book, *"bleeding flesh will heal with time, but bleeding hearts do not."* *I never really thought about it but maybe Shawn was right. Maybe I do have my own bleeding father-wound?*

I'll have to admit, I knew the pain of loneliness eating at my insides. I knew what it felt like to be abandoned and all alone. I knew the trauma of growing up without a mom. I experienced the shame of having an alcoholic dad. I felt the pain of bruises and broken bones from all the beatings.

I tried to push the thoughts away. It dawned on me that I must squarely face my own father-wound before I can ever be free to help my son. But how?

Then I remembered seeing something in the book about a retreat for fathers and sons. I picked the book up again and flipped to the Appendix, and then I saw it. An invitation to a Father's Day Retreat where dads and sons could get their broken relationships healed.

Hmmm. Maybe this could help me be a better dad. Maybe it could even help Shawn get over his hatred toward me. We both need our father-wounds healed.

INVITATION TO A RETREAT

Just then a knock came on my door. I got up and unlocked it. It was Shawn.

"Oh, good. Just the person I wanted to see. Son, I've been trying to read your book, but I just can't do it. My own boyhood was so tough that the book just makes me recall all those painful memories."

"That's the point," Shawn said with a bitter edge.

"I guess it is, but I don't like what I see in myself. I think you were right—I do have a deep father-wound. I need to get it healed, but I don't know how. I know my sister goes to a therapist to try to get over her hurt, but it costs her a fortune and I can't see it's helped her much."

I continued, "But Shawn, listen. I was looking at the end of the book and I saw this Father's Day Retreat. I think it might be good for us to go and hear the stories of other fathers and sons who've been through the same thing."

"Yeah, I saw that too, but that's way down on the gulf coast."

"I know, but that's not my hesitation. Frankly, it looks like it might be religious, and you know how I feel about that stuff."

"Dad, you have a wounded heart. You don't need religion, but you do need a relationship with Christ. I'm wounded too, but filling my life with faith in Him has helped me so much."

"Maybe this Retreat could help both of us?" I said. "I did see that we can swim in the ocean and play tennis or softball at the camp. We can roast hot dogs around the campfire. Maybe we can even get in a little surf fishing."

"I don't know... I kinda had other plans for my summer..."

Then with a final effort, I said, "It's Father's Day, Shawn. Would you do it for me?"

"Well, maybe it would be good to get away and go to the beach. Okay, I guess I'll go," Shawn said half-heartedly.

DRIVING TO THE CAMP

School ended that week and Shawn and I began preparing for our trip. As we drove, we didn't talk much. Finally, we hit Pensacola, Florida and we knew we were close. We crossed a bridge over the bay into Alabama.

Then turning south, Shawn spotted a huge stone sign that read *"AMERICA ABLAZE for the Lamb."* The moment we turned in, we noticed something different in the air.

The atmosphere, even in the car, seemed to resonate with an intangible presence. We didn't know what it was, but we could feel a heat on our faces and a tingling sensation in our hands.

We turned into the camp and drove slowly up the long driveway. Looking around, we saw fathers and sons of all ages and races scattered throughout the camp. While burgers sizzled on the grill, some of the guys shot hoops on the court, some swam in the pool, others played sand volleyball, and some sat and talked in a beautiful prayer garden under the sprawling oak trees.

Several guys ran up to our car, welcoming us and offering to help carry our gear to our beds. Everyone seemed to be excited and expectant.

We were famished, so after stuffing ourselves with thick juicy burgers, grilled veggies, potato salad, baked beans and banana pudding, we all crossed over a quaint little bridge and headed out to the chapel.

As we entered the glass doors, a worship band was already playing. We both noticed, that the thick presence we had experienced as we arrived, seemed even heavier in the chapel.

❖ ❖ ❖

REVIVAL COUNTRY

Shawn and Brad had entered revival country and they were about to be flooded with the presence of God. The main camp house was the former home of Evangelist Steve Hill. Starting on Father's Day, 1995, Steve, along with Pastor John Kilpatrick, had led one of the greatest revivals in American history.[45]

For at least five years, over four million people had come from around the world to the Brownsville Revival in Pensacola. They came because they were hungry for a genuine encounter with God. Of course, Bradley Hudson didn't come to find God; but he did come to find his son.

Now this camp, where the evangelist once lived, seemed to carry on this same spirit of revival.[46] It was wonderfully refreshing, but it was a whole new experience for this father and son.

In moments they would hear stories about young men who would lay bare their hearts and tell their stories. Most of them had been healed of their bitterness toward their dads at this camp.

I will tell you now that it wasn't the camp that healed them. It wasn't even the great staff and all the volunteers who poured out their hearts to help these fathers and sons. You are about to see what really healed their hearts, and you might just be surprised…

PART II
The Father's Day Retreat

8

Healing Fathers and Sons

True Stories of Forgiveness

Shawn and I sat glued to our chairs in the chapel. We had never been to a Christian camp like this, so we were both a bit nervous. The atmosphere in the chapel was filled with peace. A sense of reverence filled the room. The band played softly and the men seemed subdued by the presence of God in the air.

I looked around and saw the rugged wood slats illumined with blue lights and amber string lights. A massive wooden cross, reaching from floor to ceiling, captured everyone's attention. Nail holes pocked the wood where it looked like hundreds of folded papers had been nailed to the wood. I wondered what that was all about.

An older lady stepped up to the microphone and welcomed everyone with a smile. She said, "Hi Guys. I'm Dr. Sandy, the owner and director of the camp. I want you guys to know we've been praying for you by name all month. Our prayer is that each one of you will grow closer to one another as fathers and sons, and especially that you will grow closer to God."

She introduced the rest of the staff and then invited a young man named Nick to come tell us his story.

NICK'S STORY

"I came to this camp an absolute mess," Nick said. "I hated my dad for molesting me and my sister as children. I spent the next ten years numbing my pain with drugs and alcohol and sex."

"One day at the camp the leaders began ministering to our father-wounds. An older guy said to me, 'Has anyone ever repented to you for what your dad did?'"

"His question shocked me. It's like it tore off an old dirty band aid from a long-buried wound. 'No, *never!*' I burst out. Suddenly, I was filled with memories of all the abuse I suffered for so many years."

"I poured out my story to this kind man, and then he asked me if he could stand in as my dad and repent to me for what my father had done to me and my sister. His words seemed to strike the raw wound in my heart. I cried out all my anger and grief. Then he led me in a prayer to confess my hatred and forgive my dad. It was hard, but I did it."

"And guess what? A few years later I met with my dad. He was so ashamed he couldn't even look me in the eyes. I put my hands on his shoulders and said, 'I love you, Dad. You are my father and I love you unconditionally. And I forgive you.' Then, you know what happened? I led him to receive Jesus Christ!"

Now with a huge boyish grin, Nick said, "Today I'm a changed man. I married the pastor's daughter and serve as youth pastor and worship leader in my father-in-law's church."

As we listened, I had never heard stories which offered such hope. Shawn drank in every word, but I sat there, my arms folded, feeling out of place and doubtful. I know people spend lots of money on therapy, but these guys are telling us what forgiveness and a commitment to Christ can do. I wasn't so sure, but I could feel my heart beginning to slowly soften.

JUAN'S STORY

Now Juan stepped up to the mic. Juan was like a big sweet teddy bear as he told us his sad story, smiling through his tears. "My whole life I was passed around from home to home. It seemed like nobody wanted me."

Now here's a guy I can relate to, I thought. *After my mom died when I was eight years old, I always felt unwanted.*

Juan said, "When I was only three, I was accused of setting my mom's house on fire. My aunt locked me in solitary confinement in a room at her house for weeks."

"My dad heard about it and came and got me, but I was so hurt and rebellious that I only caused trouble for him and his new wife. Finally, he kicked me out of the house when I was ten. I had to walk ten miles to my mom's house, which put me back in the midst of poverty and drugs."

"I grew up to be a wounded and broken man, but when I was 36, I attended a men's retreat, thinking there has to be more. That's when I met Jesus. He loved me and forgave me and helped me forgive all those who had rejected me.

"At last, I had found the One who really wanted me." Looking out over all of us, Juan said, "Guys, that's what He wants for you, too."

RUBEN AND ADRIAN'S STORY

His story moved me deeply, and I began to realize—there must really be something to this concept of bringing old wounds into the light and forgiving our fathers. I knew I had wounded my own son, but I was beginning to see that wounded dads wound sons.

Now Ruben and his son Adrian, stood before us to share their story. Ruben said, "I was a hard-working businessman, trying to make a good living to support my family. I loved my wife and kids, but I was driven to succeed, and something went wrong when my son became a teenager."

Uh oh, this sounds so much like me and Shawn. I wonder how he will take it? I slipped a look over at him, and he seemed gripped by their story.

Ruben continued, "I didn't know what was wrong, but my boy wouldn't talk to me. He would stomp into his room, slam the door and bury himself in his dark music and violent video games."

"I just couldn't seem to get through to him. He never smiled. He never talked, and he seemed to hate me. I didn't know what to do, but I had heard great things about this camp, so I decided to give it a try. Now I want my son, Adrian, who is eighteen, to come tell you his side."

Adrian said, "When I first came to this camp, I planned to run away as soon as I got here. But my plan blew to smithereens when my dad decided to come too!"

A ripple of laughter swept through the room.

"I loved my dad, but I hated him even more. He was always making us move so he could make more money. Just when I had made new friends and was beginning to feel accepted, he would yank us away and take us to a new city."

Shawn sat straight up when he heard this. Adrian was his same age and he was telling his same story.

Adrian continued, "Yeah, he never seemed to care about how I felt. Once I had a girlfriend I really liked, but when I told her we had to move, she broke up with me. She wanted a boyfriend for her senior year."

Shawn groaned. I stole a glance at him.

"I was so mad," Adrian said. "When Dad told me we were moving again, I couldn't take it anymore. I gulped down a whole bottle of pills to try to kill myself. But just before I was about to pass out, I called my dad on my cell phone and told him I needed help."

"He rushed to my room and he and mom helped me to the car. They raced me to the hospital, trying to save my life, but I just wanted to die."

As Shawn and I sat there, I could feel the emotion rising in my boy. Adrian's story was so much like his. He had always hated me for making us move, and though he had become a Christian, he couldn't shake the anger and depression building deep within him.

Now Adrian's dad, Ruben, came forward and said, "I love my son so much, but I could not seem to break through to him. He just barricaded himself in his room and listened to his dark music. He told me later that his music fed his hatred."

I glanced again at Shawn, who leaned forward, his face beet red as he nodded knowingly.

Ruben went on. "Now here we were, rushing my son to the hospital. When we got there, I stood by his bedside. He was drifting in and out of consciousness, but I said over and over to him, 'Son, I'm so sorry. I love you. Please don't die!' I promised him that, as soon as possible, we would move back to California and never move again."

As I listened, my heart ached. This is what I had done to my own son and it broke me. My memory slipped back to that day I raised the garage door and found my son hanging from a noose. That changed my life forever. *Oh, if only my son could forgive me!*

Ruben continued, "When Adrian was finally released from the hospital, my wife said, 'Adrian, why don't you go back to that camp in Alabama, where you were so happy?'"

"I thought about it and said, 'Yeah, that's what I want to do. I want to go back and get right with God.'"

"So that's exactly what my son did. He came here to the camp where he got more of his wounds healed and where the Holy Spirit filled him full of Jesus. He renounced the dark power that filled him from all the movies and music, and some of the guys even prayed for him to be delivered from a spirit of darkness."

"Now today, my son is on fire for God! He has started two Christian clubs in his high school, he has been invited to preach and testify many times, he's done mission work overseas. I am so proud of my son!"

We all clapped when we heard how this story turned out. It gave us hope for our own lives. Ruben concluded by praying over everyone. "Now tomorrow, we want to go deeper," he said. "We want to help you with your own father-wounds."

"This can happen for you too if you want. But honestly, Guys, you have to *want* it. Nobody will push you or try to manipulate you. Maybe you've seen some of that on television, but we don't believe in it. The Holy Spirit is the one who motivates."

"So right now, we've got a big campfire roaring outside and, if you want, you can roast some hotdogs and marshmallows or just hang out for awhile."

BRAD'S STRUGGLE WITH GOD:

Shawn and I walked outside to the campfire where fathers and sons stood around talking about all the stories they had heard. Shawn gobbled down a couple of hotdogs followed by charred marshmallows, but my heart was too heavy to eat anything.

The gravity of these stories hit me hard, even though they all had such great endings. *Could it be true that God does exist, and that He can make such a profound difference in a person's life?*

I went to bed but hardly slept. I felt torn between my anger with God for all the pain He had caused in my life and the conviction I felt from some unseen force.

That age-old question tormented me—if God is real, why would He allow such suffering in the world? If there really is a God, why would be make me hurt so much? I could not reconcile this in my mind. I tossed and turned all night.

WHEN WE ARE DISAPPOINTED WITH GOD

As Bradley Hudson grapples with God, he is like so many today. Because he had experienced deep suffering as a boy, instead of drawing close to God, he had blamed Him for his pain. This has become a huge stumbling block to him, and until he gets this settled, it will hold him back.

Let's look more deeply into this struggle that Brad is having, and in the next chapter, discover what God's answer to human suffering really is.

9

No More Blaming God

What Has God Done About Human Suffering?

When I awoke in the morning, I still wrestled with my questions about God. It didn't stand to reason—if God is real, why would He allow such suffering in the world? If God exists, why would He be so cruel?

I felt torn between my anger with God for all the pain in my life and the conviction I felt from some unseen force.

But the aroma of coffee and bacon filled the morning air, and I made my way to the dining area. After a hearty breakfast, we gathered in the prayer garden beneath the sprawling oak branches.

I drew in a deep breath of the fresh country air. It was good to be away from the rat-race of the city. I could hear the breeze rustling through the leaves, birds twittering in the trees, and squirrels screeching as they chased each other across the branches.

Just then Pastor Ryan stepped out on the deck. Ryan had lived at the camp during his Brownsville Revival days, and he was one of Dr. Sandy's students. He and his wife now pastor a church in Fort Worth and he often comes down to help direct camps and retreats.

Now he was draped in a white sheet and playing the role of Jesus in a drama. He began walking among the people, reaching out his hands and speaking words of love.

Suddenly, someone jumped up and pushed Jesus away as he approached him. Loudly he shouted, "Leave me alone, Jesus! You don't care about me. Where were you when my dad cheated on my mom and left our family?"

Jesus kept reaching out lovingly. "Get away from me, Jesus. Where were you when my best friend killed himself?" Every time someone rejected him, Jesus gripped his heart and groaned.

"Yeah, and where were you when those kids got massacred in my school? Some of my closest friends died. How could you? You don't care about any of us, if you did, you wouldn't allow so much suffering!"

I sat there appalled. Everyone was blaming Jesus for their suffering, just like I've always done. *It's almost like God had read my thoughts last night. Hmmm…*

Jesus walked over to me and Shawn and reached out His arms. Shawn jumped up, slapped him in the face, leaving blood marks. "Where were you when my mom died, and my dad became an alcoholic?"

Oh, wow, Shawn is telling my story, but I've hardly told him anything about my painful past. Shawn's voice cracked as he yelled at Jesus, "I hate you! I hate you!"

Those words from my son stabbed me sharply. I could see the red streaks on Jesus' face, and I thought to myself, *It's true, I've blamed God for all the pain in my life. Even my own son sees it.*

Jesus walked a few steps and threw himself to his knees by a bench in the garden. "Oh Father, they don't understand how much I love them. They think God is the cause of all their pain, when I came to save them, not hurt them: 'The thief comes to kill, steal, and destroy, but I have come to give them life more abundantly' (John 10:10)."

This was hitting me hard. I wanted to get up and run. But for Shawn's sake, I held on.

Jesus continued, "If they could only know what I am about to do for them. I am going to the cross where I will bleed for them, I will weep for them, I will carry their sin and drink the Father's cup for them. Like a substitute lamb, I will take their place and endure the flames of punishment for them. I will take their hell so they can have our heaven!"

Suddenly, a harsh voice shouted, "There he is. Get him!" Three young men charged into the prayer garden and grabbed Jesus. They beat him and kicked him and smeared a blood-red substance on his face and chest.

They pushed him up to the cross and hammered him to the wood. All the while people in the prayer garden were yelling, "Crucify him! He doesn't deserve to live. He said he is God. See, he's nothing but a mere man!"

From the cross, Jesus cried, "Father, please forgive them; they don't know what they are doing!" He paused, then lifted up his voice and roared, "*Eli, Eli, lama sabachthani! My God, My God, why have you forsaken me?*" Then he released his spirit to the Father and slowly bowed his head.

One by one, those who had accused him, came up and fell at his feet. Shawn cried, "Oh Jesus, I am so sorry I blamed you for my mom's death. Forgive me for falsely accusing You!" Others ran up and repented to him with all their hearts.

Jesus stepped down from the cross and touched each one, saying, "I forgive you. Don't you know I saw every tear you cried alone at night? I heard every cry when your father abused you. I longed to comfort you when your best friend killed himself.

I walked through your school calling you all to myself. And when Satan entered into that crazed young man who shot up your school, I grieved with you. Don't you see? I didn't do this to you. The enemy of your soul did it."

Jesus said, "You have wondered—why does God allow human suffering?"

It almost seemed that he looked straight at me.

"I must tell you," he continued, "the question is not WHY? The question is WHAT—what has God done about human suffering?"

Then Jesus smiled and held out his arms. "Don't you see? I came down from heaven's perfect bliss to enter your world of pain and heartache. I wept for you; I bled for you; I carried all your grief and pain; I paid the price for your sin; I stood in for you and took your punishment so that, by my shed blood, you could be forgiven."

"Yes, God's answer to human suffering is the cross of His only Son. What has God done about suffering? 'He gave His one and only Son that whoever believes in Him will have everlasting life' (John 3:16)."

COMMUNION

Then stepping up on the deck, Jesus took the bread of Communion and said, "This is my body which was broken for you…. This is my blood which was shed for you. Take this to remember I am not the cause of your suffering."

As men, young and old, took the juice and the broken bread, tears rolled down many faces.

But I was still struggling. It seemed I had been struggling my whole life with this question of why God allows suffering. And now, this simple drama answered all of my questions.

I closed my eyes and silently prayed, *Jesus, forgive me for blaming You for all the terrible things in my life. I blamed you for my mom's death, for my dad's alcoholism, for my still-born baby girl, and for all the trouble I've had with Shawn, but oh, my God—it wasn't Your fault!*

In that moment, it was like lightning struck my heart. I suddenly realized who Jesus Christ is—and it broke me. I covered my face with my hands… When I finally lifted my head, all the men had left the garden. Only Shawn remained, knowing something deep was happening in my soul.

In my stubbornness, I still had not given my life to Christ, but I was seriously thinking about it.

THE GOOD SHEPHERD
LAYS DOWN HIS LIFE FOR THE SHEEP

We have enacted this drama in the streets of England and Africa and many places in America. Its purpose is to show the absurdity of blaming the One who loves you and gave His life for you.

When people yell and slap and kick Jesus, they are blaming Him for some of the cultural issues we face today, which all have roots in sin and darkness. We blame Him for dads cheating on wives, parents divorcing and wounding their kids, sexual predators abusing innocent kids, depressed teens hanging themselves or gobbling down pills, angry boys shooting up schools.

None of these tragedies are caused by God. Jesus said, "The thief comes to steal, kill, and destroy" (John 10:10). But He told us that He is the Good Shepherd who lays down His life for His sheep, and to give us "life in its fullness until you overflow!" (John 10:10-11, TPBT).

The reason Brad needed to repent to God over blaming Him for his suffering, is so that his heart will be softened and able to receive healing for his father-wound.

Now, as we continue on with our story, Brad is finally ready for his father-wound to be healed. This is indeed the first of five steps for restoring your relationship with your son. It has to begin with *you*.

10

How to Heal Your Father-Wound

The Power of Forgiveness

Shawn and I were late when we entered the chapel. Ruben was already speaking: "Last night my son Adrian and I told you our story. The key that seemed to open my son's heart was when I said sincerely, 'Son, I'm sorry I made you move all those times, uprooting you from your friends. It was so wrong for me not to consider your feelings.'

"I learned that it's not good enough to say *If* I was wrong, or *if* I hurt you. No *ifs*. It must be earnest repentance that goes straight to the heart of the hurt."

"I know we guys often think it shows weakness to apologize, but in reality, it shows great strength. It opens a son's heart when we sincerely repent. So let me ask you men in this chapel today—fathers and sons alike—has anyone ever repented to *you* for what you have been through with your father?"

He lowered his tone and softened his voice as he spoke to them as a gentle loving father. "I want to ask you now—would you allow me to stand in the place of your father and tell you how sorry I am?"

"Please close your eyes and imagine Jesus on the cross. See the compassion in His eyes, and the love in His heart as He leads you through to forgiveness. Remember that here from the cross, He forgave you, and now He asks you to forgive your dad."

"Let me stand in the place of your dad and repent to you. Picture your own father's face. Hear him saying these words to you: 'Son, I want to tell you how sorry I am that I got your mom pregnant with you before we were married." He looked out at us and said, "I know this won't apply to all of you, but I'm sorry for the shame, the bullying, and the names you were called."

With my eyes closed, I tried to imagine my father's face. But even the thought caused me to recoil. Ruben kept on, standing in as though he were my dad, repenting to each of us. He apologized for the drinking and cursing and abusive language. He repented for slapping mom and pushing her around.

He said, "I'm sure, if you had been big enough, you would have protected her from me. You were too young to fight me back, and this must have caused deep anger to build inside. Please forgive me." Ruben paused and let his words sink into the men…

"I'm so sorry for the divorce and for tearing your world apart. Your mom had to work, and this often left you alone. I know you must have felt ashamed for not having decent clothes because of your poverty. I wish I could have given you more."

Men of all ages brushed away tears. My own throat tightened as I heard him repent about the beating and the poverty and the shame and the filthy clothes. I sighed deeply but still held my emotions in check.

"I'm sorry I never taught you how to treat a woman. I never knew how myself, so I couldn't teach you. I apologize that I didn't talk to you about sex because I didn't know how in a clean way."

"I'm so sorry for all the programs I missed or the sports I never attended. Other dads were there, but I was not. This made you feel lonely and ashamed."

Shawn stiffened, fighting back the tears. His grief and shame over not having his dad at his games dug deep.

"I'm so sorry I broke my promises and hardly ever kept my word. I'm sorry I rarely, if ever, hugged you, and I never told you I loved you. That was so wrong."

"I apologize for all the birthdays I missed. I didn't forget. It brought up too much pain, and I wanted to spite your mom. But I was only thinking of how I felt."

Ruben paused again…

"I regret that I embarrassed you in front of your friends, never encouraging or affirming your masculinity. I only mocked your weaknesses, as though that would push you to improve. It was wrong."

As I listened, I felt like my heart was beginning to bleed. Never had anyone ever repented to me for the cruelty of my dad. But when I heard Ruben's next apology, I lost it.

"I am so sorry, Son, for the way I didn't protect you. I let that man abuse you, to touch you wrongly, and confuse your sexuality. I was too drunk to realize what he was doing to you…"

Suddenly I felt like my heart would burst with grief and rage. A loud bitter cry broke from my lips.

MINISTRY TO WOUNDS

At that point, Ruben knew it was time to stop and minister to our wounds. He invited the prayer team to come forward, which was made up of volunteer dads. Then he said, "I want everyone who has been wounded by your father to come up here for ministry."

Shawn quickly made his way up to the front, and I came forward too. I found an older, seasoned gentleman, to step in as my father. He introduced himself as Jim and asked me about my story.

Then he said, "Brad, tell me about the worst thing that ever happened with you and your dad."

I gasped. "The *worst?*" I groaned again and tears filled my eyes. I could barely talk as I told Jim about the most horrifying night of my life, when my father brought two drunk men home. I didn't tell him much. It was too embarrassing, but it was the first time in my life I had ever mentioned it.

"They tried to rape me and my sister. We narrowly escaped into the icy cold night. My dad never even knew it happened. He was too drunk."

"Brad, has anyone ever repented to you for that terrible experience?"

"*Nooo!*" Suddenly, the rage and fury which I had carried for many years, broke loose like an erupting volcano, spewing out its molten lava of hatred. I cried until I sobbed as the rage spilled out from within.

"I hate him! I hate him!" I yelled. I didn't fully know what was happening, but I was releasing a great mass of grief which had been buried inside me for decades.

Eventually Jim said, "Son, I'm so sorry. As your dad, I should have protected you from those men. Please forgive me."

I leaned over on Jim's chest and let it all pour out. When my heaving finally stopped, Jim said, "Are you ready now to forgive your dad?"

"I can try."

"I want you to ask Jesus where He was when those men attacked you and your sister. You see, He is eternal and timeless. The Bible says, "Jesus Christ is the same yesterday, today, and forever" (Heb. 13:8). That's why, when trauma happens, you can ask Him to walk into a terrible memory and show His love in the midst of it. He will absorb the pain from the wound. This will help you be able to forgive. Can you see where He was?"

"I see Him…He is pulling the big guy off of me…then the other one off my sister. He is helping us escape. Now He is holding us both closely during the freezing night."

Jim asked me what happened when we came home? Where is your dad?

"He's still passed out on the couch."

Jim said, "Now I want you to wake him up and speak up to him. Tell him the truth. You have felt voiceless too long."

So I did. I spoke to him about everything he had done to hurt me and abuse me and ruin my baseball and leave me and Jenny hungry and dirty.

"What else?" asked Jim.

"Dad, the thing that hurt me the most is that you didn't care when those men molested us. It was so scary, and you were passed out drunk on the couch. I hate you for that!"

"That's so good, Brad. How do you feel now?"

"I feel like I just unlocked and released all the fury and rage of a lifetime!"

Now Jim asked me, "Have you ever thought much about your own father's father-wound? Do you know anything about his relationship with his dad?"

"Yeah, in rare moments my dad would tell me how his dad used to beat his mom. And when he got older, he said he had some real knock-down-drag-outs with him. It was brutal."

"Then when my mom died, he lost it. He tried to drink his troubles away, completely neglecting me and my sister."

"Brad, can you ask Jesus how He feels about your dad? Do you think He would want you to have compassion for him and forgive him?"

"I guess so, but oh, it's so hard!"

"I know," said Jim, "But now I want you to look back up at Jesus on the cross. Remember the verse, 'If we confess our sins, He is faithful and just to forgive us our sin and to cleanse you from all unrighteousness.... And the blood of Jesus His Son cleanses us from all sin' (1 John 1:9, 7).

"Look into the face of Jesus and see His face dripping with His own blood. Then tell Him how sorry you are for that sin of bitterness which has been eating you up for years. Bring to Him the sin that has held you back for so long. Let Him wash you with His blood."

Jim then said, "Now Brad, with your eyes on Jesus, see His cleansing blood pouring out from every wound. Can you see His wounds bleeding with rich red blood? That blood is to cleanse you of all your hatred so you'll be able to forgive."

Jim waited a few minutes as I quietly mumbled my prayer. "Now, with your eyes on Him, say to the Lord, 'I am *powerless* to forgive my dad. Would you please give me the power to forgive?'"

I prayed, "Lord, I am *powerless* to forgive, but would you come and give me the power to forgive him?" I waited and when I thought I might be feeling some help from the Holy Spirit, I said, "Lord, because of what Jesus did for me, I forgive my dad."

Jim said, "What do you forgive him for?"

I started naming everything. "I forgive you, Dad, for breaking my arm and never taking me to the doctor. I forgive you for ruining all my baseball hopes…"

A few tears started escaping, and Jim said, "Good, let that grief out when you need to. Now keep going."

"I forgive you for never washing our clothes and never having food for us to eat in the morning. I forgive you for all the shame and bullying this caused for me and my sister." Again, the tears slipped down.

I went on and on, naming everything that came to me. Then I stood and breathed in the spirit of forgiveness. I honestly felt like a thousand tons of baggage were lifting off of my chest. It was crazy. I really felt free.

"One more thing," said Jim. "I know this is hard, but you need to forgive *yourself*." He held up a mirror. "Look into your own eyes because eyes are windows into the soul. Now say, 'I forgive myself.'"

I flinched, darting my eyes away.

"I know," Jim said. "Nobody likes this part, but it is so needed. Try again."

I took a deep breath and looked into my own eyes. I said, "Because Jesus forgives me, I forgive myself!" I said it twice more and then looked up smiling.

Now Jim asked me, "Brad, are you ready to give your life to Christ?"

I sighed deeply and said, "Jim, I think I want to do this, but I still have a few more things to work out with the Lord. I'm sorry, I'm still not ready yet."

"But one thing I do know—I am ready now to humble myself to my son and ask his forgiveness."

STEP ONE OF FIVE STEPS

Yes, now Brad had forgiven his dad and forgiven himself and he was ready to ask his son's forgiveness.

He has now completed the first of five steps for restoring his relationship with his son. This is the hardest part but once you've really forgiven your own dad, the rest will follow fairly easily.

Now he is ready for the second step. He will reach out to his son and repent to him for all the pain and stain of their past relationship. Hopefully his son will forgive him. But will he? It won't be easy.

11

The Courage to Say, "I'm Sorry!"

Repenting to Your Son

"We've had a pretty draining day, so let's have some fun!" said Pastor Ryan. "After lunch we have volleyball and softball games scheduled. And for those who'd like to go to the beach, it's a beautiful day, so go have a good time. But whatever you do, do it together, as fathers and sons."

Shawn and I couldn't wait to get to the beach. We lived in a landlocked state, with no opportunity for surf fishing. This was late June, the time of year when redfish, pompano, speckled trout, and Spanish mackerel are running.

SURF FISHING ON THE BEACH

Perdido Beach lay only twenty minutes away from the camp. So we jumped in our car and took off toward the beach. On our way we stopped and purchased live shrimp and fishing licenses. Then we headed over the bridge to the beach.

When we first dug our toes into the sugar-white sand and looked out over the aqua blue waters of the Gulf, the beauty almost took our breaths away. We could hardly wait to throw out our lines. A soft breeze rippled over the surface of the sea and an occasional fish splashed from the water, whetting our appetites to fish.

But I actually had something else on my mind. I said, "Let's first take a walk down the beach. I'll show you how to spot where the fish are swarming in schools. My dad taught me how to surf fish before my mom died."

I smiled as I thought of those once happy days. I had finally forgiven him, and now I found myself remembering some of the good times.

As we walked the beach, I cleared my throat and said, "Uh, Son, there's something I need to tell you. Well, actually, I need to ask you."

Shawn looked at me curiously.

"You know something happened to me today. First, in the prayer garden this morning, after that drama, when I asked the Lord's forgiveness for the way I had blamed Him for all my suffering."

"I realized now that God didn't cause those things to happen to me. I am still mulling over the concept that God's answer to human suffering is the sacrifice of His only Son."

"Then in the chapel, listening to all the stories and forgiving my own dad, I realized even more what a terrible dad I have been to you."

Shawn quietly listened as we walked along. "Honestly, Son, I never meant to hurt you. I wanted to be a great dad. But it was like I was running from something. All I wanted to do was make money and be a success. I didn't want you to suffer like I had suffered. Now I realize that true success is being a good father."

Shawn looked down, thinking about his dad's words, and trying not to react.

"So what I'm trying to say is…" I took a deep breath and said, "I've been so wrong… Son, could you please forgive me?"

Shawn didn't speak, but to himself he thought, *so he thinks he can say a few words and sweep it all away? He doesn't understand. I know I'm a new Christian, but I'm sure God understands how I feel.*

I tried to swallow down the lump in my throat. "I am sorry. Son, will you please try to find it in your heart to forgive me?" I repeated.

"I know I haven't been there for you. I apologize for blowing up over your music that night. It was wrong. I'm sorry I missed all those baseball games. I'm sorry I've been so full of pride and selfishness. . ."

Shawn remained silent for a long time. A fish leapt and flopped from the water, diverting our attention. Finally, my son couldn't contain his feelings any longer.

His face flushed with anger and he cried, "Dad, I hated you when you forced us to move all those times. Just when I had made new friends, and just when I was part of a baseball team, and when I finally felt like I belonged, you ripped up our roots and made us move again."

All I could do now was shake my head and say, "I'm sorry. I'm so sorry."

Shawn's fists tightened and his voice rose, "And why didn't you come to any of my games? There was one game when I pitched a no-hitter and received the Most Valuable Player award. Where were you then?" He wiped away the hot, angry tears. "All the other dads were there. I was so hurt and ashamed!"

"Son, could you find it in your heart to forgive me?"

"It's not that easy. You can't make up for lost time. You can't just come to a retreat and suddenly expect me to forgive you, like nothing happened."

Shawn turned suddenly and shouted, "I'm going fishing!" He stomped angrily back to the spot where we had left our ice chest with shrimp and bottled waters. He baited his hook and cast it as far out as he could.

"Lord, I'm sorry," Shawn prayed. "I didn't really want to come to this retreat. This was his idea. Now I feel like I have to forgive, but I'm just not ready."

I trudged back to our fishing spot with my own gear. I baited my line with a shrimp and cast it out. I stole a quick glance at Shawn, but I could see he was still brooding.

After several more casts, I shouted over to Shawn, "Let's go find where the fish are biting. I still want to show you how to tell when a school of pompano or reds are passing by."

We walked silently for a few hundred yards. Suddenly, I pointed out to sea and said, "Look! Do you see those churning waters out there? Oh, my gosh, look, Shawn. It's blowing up right out there about thirty to forty feet!"

They quickly baited their hooks again and cast as far as they could. Instantly, a fish hit Shawn's line. "Hold steady, Son. Give it a jerk to set the hook, now reel it in as fast as you can... That's good...Don't give your line any slack or he might wiggle off your hook."

The fish fought for his very life, and Brad encouraged his son all the way. "C'mon. You can do it! That's the idea. You got him now!"

Finally, Shawn heaved his fish up to the shore. I shouted, "Oh man, look at that! It's a beautiful pompano, probably 16–18 inches!"

"Wow! that's a keeper!" yelled Shawn proudly. I snapped a picture and sent it over to Shawn's phone. Shawn's excitement showed all over him. He was like a little kid again. We chucked the fish into our ice cooler, and for the next hour or so, we pulled the fish in as fast as we could cast out our lines.

When we finally reached our legal limit, we sat down on the sand, exhausted from a phenomenal day of fishing. We grabbed two bottles of water out of the ice chest, now laden with redfish, speckled trout and pompano. The successful catch had lightened both of our moods.

We sat in silence until finally Shawn spoke up. "I guess I've been a real jerk. I know it took a lot of guts for you to apologize, but this is really hard for me, Dad. I know I need to forgive you because God forgave me, but I'm just not there yet."

I nodded my head in understanding.

CALMING THE STORM IN YOUR SON

This then is the second step in a five-step process for reaching your son. This second step is asking your son's forgiveness, essentially repenting to him.

Before we continue with this story, let me ask you—what would you do if you were in Bradley's shoes. Would you be able to take the words of anger and rage without defending and striking back? It will take real maturity not to blaze back at your son. How dare he talk to you, his father, like that!

But remember, Shawn has been holding this bitterness inside for a long time. This inner turmoil drove him into depression. It thrust him into suicide and drugs and drinking. It almost led him to blow up his school. This is the kind of violent anger that compels our broken boys to do crazy things.

He needs a dad who can help him calm the storm within him. Of course, not all boys express themselves so outrageously. Many of them internalize it and become depressed. This may even lead to suicide in our precious broken boys.

Again, I'm not saying it's all a father's fault. Shawn fed his own anger with all the dark movies and music and video games. He may have heightened his frustrations with drugs and alcohol. He may have released his emotions through pornography. But this is what is happening to our young men today.

Many of them are furious. And remember what the facts show: the root—the deep driving cause above all other causes is—*fatherlessness*. Even if you were in the home, if you weren't there for your son, he feels fatherless.

So please be willing to "turn the other cheek" and let him spew out the mania that rages within him. Then, while biting your tongue and praying for help, speak softly back to him. Remember, "A soft answer turns away wrath" (Proverbs 15:1).

Here is what Brad answered back: "I understand. I would feel the same way, but would you mind if I tell you a story?"

Now Brad is ready for the third step in *Reaching the Heart of Your Son*. He will tell him his own father-wound story. This is not for sympathy, not for an excuse, not to blame his own dad. He will tell it hopefully to soften Shawn's heart, and help him understand. And finally, to help him *forgive*.

12

The Power of Telling Your Story

Opening Your Son's Heart

The sun sank lower over the western sky, causing shimmers of golden light to gleam across the surface of the water. Here at ocean's edge, all that could be heard were the cawing of seagulls and the roar of waves rising and swelling then spilling, plunging, crashing and surging onto the shore.

My son and I sat in the wet sand, our legs stretched out in the surf, still basking in our successful catch. As the foam of the whitecaps bubbled and fizzled over our feet, I opened my heart to tell my story to my son.

"It's so hard to talk about this, Shawn, but I know you're old enough to understand." My voice trembled. "I'm not looking for pity, and I'm not trying to blame your grandpa. I take full responsibility for my failure, but I just want you to hear my story."

Shawn nodded.

"As you know, my mom died when I was eight and my little sister, Jenny, was seven. After we buried her, my dad was out almost every night, often staggering in drunk with a woman on his arm. They would disappear into the bedroom, and they both slept until long after we had left for school."

Taking a deep breath, he continued. "Every day we rummaged through piles of filthy, smelly clothes, trying to find something to wear to school. We scrounged for something to eat before catching the bus, but usually we had to go to school hungry."

"If I ever dared to complain, Dad would fly into a rage, hitting me, pushing me into furniture, and leaving me bruised and bleeding. Once he threw me off the back porch and I landed on my arm. My arm shattered and the pain was excruciating. My dad just sneered and told me to "suck it up." He locked me out of the house all night, but he never took me to a doctor, so it didn't set right. That ended my baseball dreams."

"I don't mean to make an excuse, but every time you mention your baseball to me, I feel that familiar knife twisting in my gut. Maybe that's the reason why."

Shawn gasped. "Oh, Dad, I didn't know!" He could feel the tears filling his heart and pushing against his eyelids. He could not imagine how terrible it would be to lose his baseball career because of a father's abuse. He swallowed hard and listened with increased interest.

I furrowed my brow and said, "I always swore that I would be a good dad and I would provide well for my children so you wouldn't have to go without. I know I failed you because I haven't given you what you wanted most—the love of a father—but, Shawn, I didn't know how."

Shawn blinked and a tear darted down his cheek. I knew he still resented me, but it seemed like my story was softening his heart.

"The worst experience of my life was when Dad brought a few nasty drunk guys home. They looked at me and my little sister, Jenny, like we were fresh meat to satisfy their sick pleasure. They waited until Dad was so drunk he didn't know what was going on. Then one of them grabbed Jenny, pushed her to the floor, started pulling off her clothes and pawing her.

"You are the first person I've ever told this whole story to. I was always too ashamed, and it hurt too much to think about it. The only reason I can tell you now is because today I was able to experience some deep healing for this terrible memory. It was like someone reached in and pulled out a huge mass of grief from my soul."

"Dad, that 'Someone' would have been the Holy Spirit."

"Well, maybe. Anyway, when that filthy man pushed my sister to the floor, the blood rushed to my head and I couldn't even think. This was my baby sister. Since my mom died and my dad went off the rails, I felt like her protector."

"But just then the other guy jumped me and started slipping his hands down my pants. I saw red. I blew up. Suddenly, I seemed to have the strength of a tiger. I kicked him so hard he was incapacitated."

I smiled as I thought back on my sudden surge of manly strength. "Then I had to rescue my little sister, so I took a baseball bat and smashed the other guy in the head. For all I know, I might have killed him, but I never heard what happened. I grabbed Jenny and we ran out into the night, barefoot and freezing."

"I don't think she ever got over the terror of that night. Neither did I. But my deepest hurt was with my dad, not the two men. He never even seemed to know that anything was wrong. He slept through it all because he was so stinkin' drunk."

I paused and looked back out over the breakers, rising and falling and pulling the tide out to sea. Finally, I lifted my head and smiled. "But do you know what happened to me today? It all started when Jim, the older guy who helped me, said, "Brad, what is the worst thing you ever experienced with your dad?""

"I told him a shortened version of my story. Then he asked, 'Has anyone ever repented to you for that terrible experience?' His question knocked the wind from my lungs."

"'Nooo!' I practically screamed. I never had anyone tell me they were sorry for what happened to me. Suddenly, the rage burst loose like a volcano, erupting and pouring out streams of burning hatred. 'I hate him! I hate him!' I wailed."

"When I finally poured out all my pain in his fatherly arms, I knew I must forgive my dad. Yet how? I didn't think I could."

"Jim then asked me about my dad's own father-wound. That's when I realized that my father's dad was actually an abusive alcoholic too. On top of that wound, when my father's wife—my mom—died, he simply couldn't handle the pain. He turned to alcohol to comfort him, instead of to God."

"You know it was so hard to forgive my dad. But I think I did."

I turned to look at Shawn with pleading eyes. With all the sincerity of my heart, I softly asked, "Shawn, won't you please find it in your heart to forgive me?"

My heart filled with hope when I saw the flood of tears dripping shamelessly down his cheeks. I reached over and slipped an arm over his shoulder. He fell into my arms and sobbed like a little boy.

When at last his tears subsided, he whispered, "Yes, Dad, I forgive you. With all my heart I forgive you!"

"Thank you, Son," I whispered brokenly. It took me a moment to recover from the shock and joy of his sudden forgiveness. The salty spray splashing on my face mingled with my tears as I looked back out to sea. Since the day I found my son hanging from a noose in the garage, I had dreamed of this moment. Now I wanted to embrace it and soak in it and let it wash over my heart like a rising, swelling, healing wave.

Finally, I managed to speak, "I'm so thankful, Son. You know I love you like I never dreamed I could love a child." My words came from the depths of my soul.

"Dad, that's all I ever wanted. I just needed to know you really love me."

I breathed out a long deep sigh of relief. We sat together in silence, watching the gulls squawking and dipping for minnows.

Finally, Shawn broke the silence. He gathered his emotions and said sincerely, "Dad, I… I want you to know how sorry I am that I hurt you, too. I'm sorry that I tried to kill myself. I'm sorry for the pain this caused you. No father should ever have to bury his son."

"Oh, Son…you'll never know. I couldn't bear to lose you. I almost did one other time. Have I ever told you what happened at your birth?"

"LIVE, SON, *LIVE!*"

"I will never forget that harrowing moment in the hospital. You were already emerging into this world, when suddenly your heart rate dropped so low, the monitor hardly registered it.

"Your mom and I were frantic, afraid it would be another still birth like your little sister. I feel the dizziness even now when I think about it. I almost fainted."

"The residents placed a breathing tube down your throat and began massaging your little body. That's when something came over me. I stepped up and placed my hand on your little chest. I said as boldly as I could, 'Shawn Michael, I am your father, and I am telling you now to breathe. As your daddy, I am commanding you to 'Live, Son, LIVE!'"

"That's when your heart began to beat more rhythmically. You caught your breath and let out a loud piercing scream. It was the most beautiful sound in the world! When at last I was allowed to hold you, I could almost feel your little heart beating against my chest. I kept thinking—*this is my son!*"

Suddenly, Shawn gasped. "Oh, my gosh, Dad, do you know what else? Do you remember when I almost killed myself and the paramedics were carrying me to the ambulance?"

"How could I ever forget. It was the worst day of my life."

"I was dying. I felt myself leaving my body and I wanted to go. All my strength had left me, but I heard your voice."

"I had forgotten this until now. But I felt your strong hand upon my chest, and I heard you calling out to me. You were telling me you loved me and begging me not to die. Suddenly, you cried with a passion like I had never heard from you—'Live, Son! LIVE!'"

"Yes, of course I remember. Just like at your birth, immediately the heart monitor picked up a steady heartbeat and you lived!"

"Dad, do you realize what I'm trying to tell you? Your voice called me back! Somehow through the fog of my comatose state, I knew you cared about me. I thought you wouldn't care if I died, but suddenly, I knew you really loved me. Your love called me back to life. It gave me the will to live."

"That experience woke me up. I never knew I could love a child so much!"

Shawn beamed and said, "Dad, that's all I ever wanted to know."

Father and son sat basking in the receding surf, watching the electric power of the waves shoot white spray high into the air. It was almost as though all our heartache and pain swept gently out to sea as the surf flowed back to its source in the ocean.

After awhile, Shawn blurted, "Hey Dad, I'm hungry! Aren't they grilling steaks tonight? We'd better get back to the camp." We packed up our gear and carried our ice chest to the car. Then we hurried back to the camp, planning to put our haul in the freezer and take it back home when we leave.

After a delicious steak dinner, we gathered back in the chapel. Pastor Ryan said, "I know you've had a great time today. And we will be having our traditional 'Overflowing Hearts' tomorrow. That's when some of you will share your stories about what God has done in your lives this weekend.

But right now, let's break into small groups of six to eight guys. We want you to share your stories. Each group needs to be sure everyone gets a chance to share. Then let's all meet back here in two hours.

By the excited chatter going on in all the groups, it was obvious that the men had a lot to share. When they all finally wandered back into the chapel, Ryan made a final announcement.

"Tomorrow morning Dr. Sandy is going to tell you about the Father's cup. This will show you the deepest reason why so many have been healed at this camp. Our healing came from the cross."

"But it's late now and we've had a full day, so if any of you are hungry, let's go out to the campfire and roast some hotdogs and marshmallows and get to bed."

STEP #3 IN REACHING YOUR SON

Now do you see the power of telling your story? It will help your son understand you and forgive you for your mistakes. Shawn needed to know the real reason why his dad avoided his ball games. And Brad needed to get in touch with what was holding him back.

Now with both of their father-wounds healed, they will be able to enjoy Shawn's baseball games together, if he continues to play.

We have two more powerful steps that need to take place. But first, in our next chapter, we will go back into the prayer garden to discover the primary reason so many have been healed at our camp. The secret is in the cross.

13

Gazing into the Father's Cup

When God Reached Down...

As we gathered again in the prayer garden, I could feel the anticipation in the air. Dr. Sandy couldn't wait to tell us about the real secret of why so many young men and women have forgiven their dads and have been healed at the camp. As Ryan said, "the healing is in the cross."

"I want to begin by telling you a personal story," she said. "During World War II, a young father, training to be an Airforce pilot, decided to take his first-born baby girl swimming in the Atlantic. Although flags warned of an approaching hurricane, he was a great swimmer, so no worries."

"That baby girl was me, and I was oblivious to the impending danger. As my dad waded out to sea, holding me in his arms, he suddenly looked up and his heart almost stopped. There, towering above us was a gigantic tidal wave. As the wave broke over us, my dad held me tightly, but the force of the violent water washed me right out of his arms. I was gone."

"Frantically, he searched crying out, screaming my name, and thrashing through the churning waters and seaweed and sand. All of a sudden, he reached out and felt a little hand. He grabbed it and pulled me to him. I sputtered and coughed and gasped for air. Crying my little lungs out, I clung to my daddy with all my might."

As I listened to her true story of near death, I was spellbound. We all were.

Now she said, "Guys, my father reached down and saved me, but this is a picture, a metaphor, of your heavenly Father reaching down to save you. He did it by sending His Son to a cross."

"So let me ask you—have you ever shed a tear over what Jesus did for you at Calvary? This was the greatest event that had ever taken place in heaven or in earth, but have you ever let it touch your heart? I know I hadn't. I had cried more tears over the death of my dog than over the death of my Lord."

"Now let me tell you my story. I was a young Bible teacher and I loved teaching the deep secrets of the Old Testament, but I thought the cross was too dry and elemental to teach. Oh, I had no idea!"

"One day my pastor suggested I read the works of Jonathan Edwards, who is considered America's greatest theologian and the man God used to ignite America's First Great Awakening."

"I began devouring his works, and I discovered an obscure sermon by Edwards entitled 'Christ's Agony.' It was based on Luke 22, when Jesus prayed in an olive orchard the night before His crucifixion. It unveiled the mystery of the cross. My heart has never stopped burning since I read that sermon."

A METHODIST CLASS

"A few weeks later I visited a Methodist Sunday School class. The people were discussing the purpose of the cross. 'Lots of people have died on crosses and we don't worship them,' said one skeptical man. 'I don't see what's the big deal about the cross!'"

"The class rose to Jesus' defense, telling about the rejection of His people, the pain of the whip and thorns, the torture of spikes hammered through hands and feet, and the bearing of our sin."

"But I was sitting there, knowing there is so much more. Jonathan Edwards had taken me into the garden of crushed olives where Jesus prayed beneath a full Passover moon. He prayed so earnestly that blood oozed out of His skin. Heavy clots of blood saturated His robe, His hair, His face, His whole body."[47]

"Why does He sweat clots of blood? His prayer tells us: 'Father, if it's possible, please remove this cup!'[48] What is this cup? Do you know what is in it? Have you ever heard a sermon about it? The Bible describes it as 'the wine of God's fury which has been poured full strength into the cup of his wrath' (Rev. 14:10)."

"No wonder blood squeezes from His heart and presses out of His skin! He has been looking into the mystery of the Father's cup and seeing the flames of wrath that await him on the cross."

"In fact, Edwards said that He would endure 'the very pains of hell,' not *after* the cross but *on* the cross. The contents of this cup were 'fully equivalent to the misery of the damned, for it was the wrath of the same God.' I could hardly believe it!" she cried. "He endured my hell! That's why Edwards said, 'His principal errand for coming to earth was to drink that cup.'"[49]

"That day a theological revolution had exploded in my heart.

I realized that the reason I had so little passion for the cross is because I had never really looked into the Father's cup. Now I was gazing into the Father's cup and my spirit was blazing."

"But here I am, sitting in this Methodist class, listening to people talk about the reason for the cross. My heart was thumping hard in my chest, knowing I needed to speak up. I was only a visitor, so I hesitated to express myself as passionately as I felt. Finally, I could hold back no longer. I opened my heart and began pouring out about the Father's cup of wrath."

"My voice vibrated as I said, 'It wasn't just the pain of the Roman scourge with its bits of bone and metal that tore His flesh to shreds. It wasn't just the thorns that pierced His brow, nor the spikes that drilled Him to the cross. It wasn't the fear of rejection from the people he loved and came to save. It was all this but so much more. In fact, this only scratches the surface."

"Think what it was like when suddenly the sky turns black and God pours all your pornography and adultery and sexual sin, all your hatred and rage and bitterness and anger toward your dad, all your pride and jealousy and drunkenness and violence—down on the innocent Son of God."

Most of us squirmed when she said this. Then she added with rising intensity, "Most of all—think what it was like when wave after wave of God's holy judgment burned down on the innocent Lamb. His one and only beloved Son was consumed in the fire of God's wrath against sin."[50]

"Why? Because He was the Substitute Lamb, taking our punishment for sin: 'The punishment that brought us peace was upon Him' (Is. 53:5, NIV)."[51]

By now I was gripped by Dr. Sandy's message. I had no idea that this was what God's Son actually did on the cross. Now, suddenly, I understood why Jesus Christ is the only way to God. No other religion has a Savior who suffered my punishment for sin. In my place, as Shawn keeps telling me.

I peeked a look at Shawn. His face blushed red and his whole body rocked back and forth. He was completely absorbed with the truth of the Father's cup.

She continued, "Most unbearable to Jesus was when the Father lifted His presence from Him. Even in His deepest suffering, as He engulfed the Father's cup of wrath against sin, the Holy Spirit departed from Him. When He could no longer bear this suffering alone, He lifted His voice and bellowed that cry, "*My God, My God, why have You forsaken Me?*"

"Scholars say this cry was shrieked with a deep, guttural, animal-like roar." That's when Dr. Sandy shocked us all by taking a deep breath and shouting with a heart-shaking roar: "*MY GOD, WHY HAVE YOU FORSAKEN ME?*"

"Of course, that day in the Methodist class, I didn't give that loud roaring cry, but I sure wanted to because that's what Jesus did. And oh, how my heart trembled as I spoke. I could feel the fire of the Holy Spirit burning down upon me. It was like nothing I had experienced in my whole life. I had been baptized in the Holy Spirit for many years, but this was more of Him than I had ever encountered. It was just like John the Baptist said, 'He will baptize you with the Holy Spirit and *fire*' (Luke 3:16)."

"I can tell you that this flame in my heart has lasted for over thirty years. I've discovered that this fire attends the message of the Father's cup. It is the heart of the gospel. It's the fire of the cross!"

She continued, "As I sat in church that day, still feeling the heat, I silently wept before God, repenting for all the other subjects I had taught through the years. These subjects were good, but in comparison to Jesus and His cross and resurrection, they were like the light of a candle swallowed up in the glory of the sun. They were peripheral subjects, not central, and they didn't carry the fire from heaven upon them."

"That day I made a promise to God. I committed to Him that for the rest of my life I would teach and preach and write about Jesus, His cross, and the gospel. At the time, I didn't realize that Paul made the same resolution: 'I determined to know nothing among you except Jesus Christ and Him crucified' (1 Cor. 2:2)."

"That was over thirty-five years ago, and I have dedicated my whole life to teaching this message. The fire that I experienced that day has never dimmed, and I have seen it burn in many others."

"Through the years, I've seen students and pastors and leaders in Africa and Nicaragua and Germany and Hong Kong and Indonesia, and so many more countries, on their knees, weeping to God, repenting for neglecting the Father's cup. Even though many were pastors who had preached the gospel for years, when they saw the contents of this cup and heard this poignant cry, the fire in their hearts flamed brighter."

"This is indeed why we have seen the healing of so many fatherless teens and young adults, not to mention all the older adults, who have come to our camp. They are willing to forgive their own dads because Jesus drank the Father's cup to forgive them. Even more, they are willing to cling tightly to the cross because Jesus has become the father they never had."

"And so, Brothers, do you see? This is the mystery of the Father's cup. It's the secret of the cross. And once you've seen it, everything will change. It gives you a burning purpose to serve Him. It stirs a holy passion for Jesus. It empowers you to forgive the ones who have hurt you."

"Furthermore, it gives meaning to Old Testament Scriptures, unveiling the mysteries of the burnt offering, the sin offering, and especially the Passover Lamb."

"You see, just as the flawless Passover Lamb was skinned and lifted on a pole, Jesus, the perfect Lamb of God, was skinned by the Roman scourge and lifted up on the pole of the cross. And even as the lamb was roasted over the flames, Jesus was roasted over the flames of God's wrath. This was His baptism of fire" (Luke 12:50).[52]

GOD REACHES DOWN…

As Dr. Sandy began to close her message, she said, "I started this morning with the story of my father reaching out his hand and lifting me out of turbulent waters."

"Now I want to tell you the rest of my story. When I was a little over two years old, I looked up at my dad while he was shaving and asked, "Daddy, who is God?" He quickly squashed my question. "Hush! We don't talk about that!" I soon learned that my parents were atheists and 'religion' must never be mentioned."

One day, when I was thirteen, I sat in a crowd of thousands and heard Howard Butt, Jr., in the style of Billy Graham, preach that

Jesus is the only way to God. At the end he gave a call to 'Come and receive Christ.'"

"My heart started pounding so hard I thought my ribs might break. I desperately wanted to go forward, but I knew I couldn't. I was too filthy to receive a holy God, even though I wanted Him more than anything in the world. So, I promised Him that I will go home and pray all day and try to get clean enough to come back tomorrow and receive Christ."

"Then I heard a song. The choir was singing it and it caught my attention. The words to the second verse blew my heart wide open:

> *Just as I am and waiting not*
> *to rid my soul of one dark blot;*
> *To Thee whose blood can cleanse each spot*
> *O Lamb of God, I come, I come.*[53]

Suddenly I knew that I didn't have to wait. This song told me His blood would wash me clean. So I rushed forward to sincerely pray to receive Christ. Now I've been devoted to Him for my whole life.

As I listened to Dr. Sandy's story, it touched some-thing deep inside me. And now she said softly, "I have a question for you. As you've been looking at the Lamb today, seeing His blood and the cup He drank for you, do you sense the Father reaching out His hand to you?"

Her question made me think. *All this time I've been resisting God.* My heart began to race as I realized, *He has healed my son and He has helped me forgive my dad, and yet, I have still resisted giving my life to Him.*

Now I thought my heart would beat right out of my chest. It was hammering so hard, I figured everyone could hear it.

Dr. Sandy continued, "So I simply want to ask you guys, with absolutely no pressure, because only the Holy Spirit can draw you to Jesus..."

"But if right now, your heart is pounding and you sense the Holy Spirit drawing you to receive Jesus as your Savior, or re-dedicate your life to Him, will you slip up here to the foot of the cross and give your life to Christ?"

I was the first one out of my seat. I almost knocked down some of the benches in the garden in my haste to get to the cross. And here on bended knee I prayed my way to the Savior, knowing I would never turn back.

As I prayed, I felt the touch of someone near me. From the corner of my eye I could see it was Shawn. He placed his hand upon my back and whispered in my ear. I dissolved in tears when he said, *"Live, Dad, live!"*

❖ ❖ ❖

IT'S ALL IN THE CROSS

People often ask me, "Why are so many healed and set on fire at your camp?" I always say—it's not the camp, it's not our five steps, it's not me, and it's not our great team.

It's the cross. It's the love of God poured out at Calvary. Jesus drank down every drop of the Father's cup, but He did it all for love. And His Father did it all for love as well: "For God so loved... that He gave His one and only Son" (John 3:16). And now, with our hearts bursting with love, we can forgive our dads and live in the freedom of the Fathers unending love.

14

Overflowing Hearts

Immersed in Water and the Holy Spirit

As Shawn and I entered the chapel, we heard several guys testifying about how the Father's cup had impacted them. Colton, a young father from Texas, said, "My life has been forever changed by what I thought I already knew about the cross."

Now Thomas, one of the leaders, came up to the mic. Tattoos covered him from neck to knees. Apparently, he had led a pretty rough life and we learned it was because of his father-wounds. He told us how he had forgiven his dad at the camp, but when he learned about the Father's cup, it blew away all his doubts and threw his heart wide open.

"I gotta tell you guys what happened after I learned about the cup. I was so excited when I left the camp that I told everyone I met about the cup. To the lady in the airport store, to the passenger next to me on the plane, to the my wife at home, to my boss at work—I asked, 'Have you heard about the Father's cup?' They all said, 'No,' so I poured out to each of them all about the cup."

One night I preached about the Father's cup in a little church. The Lord showed me that someone there was struggling with suicide. I gave that word of knowledge and then launched into my message."

"When I finished, a former Muslim, who had been saved at Teen Challenge, told me, 'I was the one who was planning to hang myself because I am so depressed from losing my wife and family.'"

"He wiped away a tear and then said, 'But when I heard you describe the Father's cup of punishment that Jesus drank in my place, I felt the spirit of suicide and depression lift off of me!'"

"I saw him a few weeks later," Thomas said, "and he was still free!"

BAPTISMS

Thomas released us to go to lunch, reminding us that we will have baptisms after we eat. "I promise you—this will be one of the highlights of this retreat!"

Shawn could hardly wait. He had never been baptized, and he knew this must be important. I had been baptized as a boy, before my mom died, but I felt like I needed to be baptized again. This time I knew my heart would be in it.

Everyone gathered around the pool to support their brothers. Ryan said, "We'd like for you to make your own personal proclamation to the Lord, before we lower you into the water." He read the passage from Romans 6:1-11 and said, "This shows you that the purpose of baptism is for you to be baptized into the *death*, *burial*, and *resurrection of Christ*."

One by one, those who wanted to be baptized, walked slowly into the pool. Each one lifted his voice to heaven, crying out his commitment to God: "Father, for the rest of my life I will seek to know only Jesus Christ and Him crucified!" Another cried, "Jesus, thank you for forgiving me and giving me a new purpose and a new life. I want to live to bring You the reward of Your suffering!" It was an exhilarating, faith-building, and deeply moving experience for all of us.

Finally, it was Shawn's turn. He slipped into the water, raised his hand to heaven and shouted with all his heart, "Jesus, thank you for the cross!" … His voice broke and he waited to recover. "Thank You for healing me with my dad!" … Again, his voice cracked… "Thank you for taking all my anger and pain… Now I promise You that for the rest of my life, I will follow You!"

Sitting nearby, I thought my heart would burst. Slowly the pastors lowered Shawn into the water, and when he came out, he could literally feel the Holy Spirit filling his whole being. He stood in the water and breathed in this wonderful presence of God. Trembling from head to toe, the men had to help him out of the pool.

I came right behind him. As I entered the water, I was overcome by what I had heard from my son. Shawn sat by the steps of the pool, wrapped in a towel, still vibrating under the power of God.

I lifted my face to heaven and cried, "Jesus, thank You for saving me! And thank You for giving me back my son! Please help me become the greatest dad I can ever be. Now, for the rest of my life I will live for you and serve you with all of my heart!"

Shawn stood up, cheering me on. He watched as I was lowered into the water and came back up, my face aglow with the Spirit. Shawn couldn't hold back. He jumped into the water and met me with open arms. Still trembling with God's presence, he hugged me.

Suddenly, it was as though heaven opened and the Holy Spirit fell on both of us. We were so undone with the presence of God that we had to be assisted from the pool. It reminded everyone of Jesus' baptism when "heaven was opened and the Holy Spirit descended upon Him" (Luke 3:21-22, NASB).

HEARTS OVERFLOWING

All afternoon, while fathers and sons played sports or just relaxed, the smoky aroma of meat roasting outside filled the camp. After a huge "Meat-lovers Meal," we all filed respectfully into the chapel for "Overflowing Hearts."

Several fathers and sons were chosen to give their testimonies. Shawn and I were asked to speak last. When our time came, we walked up front together, but I spoke first. It was hard for me to tell all this, but I knew I needed to be real. I started out:

"My driving ambition to climb the ladder of success came to a sudden halt the day I raised the garage door and found my son hanging from a rope…"

A collective gasp filled the whole chapel. Men leaned forward in their chairs, listening intently. Many dads knew their own sons had been suicidal. Many sons knew of their own attempts.

I was too choked up to speak, so I handed the mic to Shawn. He said, "All I ever wanted was a father who believed in me and loved me. I resented my dad for making us move every few years. And I was hurt and ashamed that he never came to my baseball games."

"But Guys, I didn't know…" Shawn took in a deep breath and tried to steady his emotions. "I didn't know that when my dad was a star baseball pitcher, his own father, in a drunken rage, blew up and threw him off the back porch. The fall shattered the bone in his arm, but his dad mocked him for crying. He never took him to the doctor so his arm never healed right. That ended his baseball dreams."

I spoke up now. "Honestly Guys, I didn't know that's what was eating me. I didn't know that the reason I was so driven was because I was running from my own father-wound. I don't want to make excuses, but when my mom died and dad began to come home drunk with a different woman every night, my sister and I had to fend for ourselves. He was either drunk or sleeping off a binge."

"One terrifying night he brought home two filthy drunk men who took one look at me and my sister, and I knew what they wanted. They tried to rape us both, but we escaped. The part that hurt me most was that my dad was too drunk to even notice."

Now Shawn said, "But I didn't know all this. He just always kept it locked inside and chased the almighty dollar. Then one day, I couldn't take it anymore. I took a rope and put a noose around my neck to hang myself in the garage. I leapt from the ladder, but just as I was falling, the garage door opened."

"My dad raced in to get a report he'd forgotten, but suddenly he stopped, horrified. He looked at me hanging from a rope, choking and gagging, and in that moment our eyes met."

"I never told you this, Dad, but an overwhelming regret hit me as I looked into your eyes. I tried to call your name, but it was too late. Everything went black. I passed out, but I somehow awakened hearing you shout, 'Shawn, please don't die! I love you!' You laid your hand on my chest and commanded, 'Live, Son, live!'"

I said, "Oh, Brothers, you can never know what it's like to find your son like that. I had nightmares for months, but it woke me up.

So that's why we came to this retreat. I didn't want to hear any religious stuff, so I've been resisting God the whole time. I didn't come here to find God; I came here to find my son."

"I didn't know I had so much bitterness in my heart toward my own dad. Finally, I was able to forgive my father here in the chapel, and I repented to Shawn on the beach. I poured out my heart in repentance to him, but he wouldn't receive it. Then when I told him my own father-wound story, something inside him opened. He wept for me. *My Son cried for me!*"

"Finally, he looked at me and said, 'Dad, now I understand. With all my heart I forgive you.' Then in a few moments he said sincerely, 'Will you please forgive me for hating you and rejecting you and trying to kill myself?'"

"Oh, I tell you, it was wonderful! I know big boys don't cry, but *big men do!* We fell into each other's arms and sobbed like little boys! In that moment it was like all our hurt and bitterness washed out to sea on the undertow of the tide."

"There's even more," I said brightly. "This morning in the prayer garden, when I heard about the Father's cup, it hit me with a thud. My heart started thumping so hard I could hardly breathe."

"I just never could get it before, but my eyes opened when I looked into that cup. Suddenly, I knew that Jesus Christ really is the only way to the Father. No other religion has a Savior who drank the Father's cup! No other 'god' has a son who took my hell!"

"Now, I know that God is not the cause of my suffering, but He took my suffering on himself. Even more, He took all my hatred and shame and pride, and He was punished for me!"

"That's when Sandy gently called us to come to Christ. She said, 'If your heart is beating hard and you sense the Holy Spirit drawing you...'"

"Oh, I tell you, my heart was roaring. I rushed forward and fell on my knees at the foot of the cross. I gave my whole life to Christ and asked Him to come and live in me. Then I felt a hand on my back, and I knew that it was Shawn. He bent over and whispered in my ear. His words dissolved my heart in tears. He said, *"Live, Dad, Live!"*"

The men were deeply moved, responding with a loud corporate sigh of "Amen!"

I started to sit down, but Shawn, with a huge smile, said, "Wait, Dad."

Wanting to bring a little levity into our serious testimony, Shawn said, with tongue in cheek: "So look what God did when my dad finally repented to me!"

Suddenly, flashing up on the screen in the chapel, was the picture of himself holding up his 16-inch pompano fish! The next picture came up, showing him holding up a whole stringer of redfish, speckled trout and pompano!

The men in the chapel jumped up and gave a standing ovation! A perfect ending to a great story and a wonderful day.

THE FIRST THREE STEPS

In retrospect, we have seen Bradley Hudson receive healing for his own deep father-wound. This was the first step in *Reaching Your Son's Heart*.

Secondly, he humbled himself to his son and repented to him for all the ways he had failed him as a father. He could have waited for his son to repent to him, but instead, he took the initiative and apologized for his failure. And when his son blew up at him, he didn't defend himself or get angry; nor did he give up.

Instead of punching back, he spoke back softly. He didn't know he was using biblical wisdom, for "A soft answer turns away wrath" (Prov. 15:1). He simply said, "Can I tell you a story?"

Too many fathers give up once they've made their apology. No! Your son must forgive you, too, or it is incomplete. Bradley kept on trying by taking the third step for reaching his son's heart.

He told him his own personal story—his father-wound story. He wasn't looking for sympathy, but he was hoping his son's heart would open up. And it did. It melted him wide open and he was able to forgive his dad. They were reconciled!

But notice that Brad didn't demand an apology from his son. He simply told him a story, and the Holy Spirit worked on Shawn's heart.

Now, in the next chapter, as we look at step four and five, we'll see that these last two steps are vital for completing the restoration between a father and a son. This is something a young man rarely, if ever, receives from his dad, but something he deeply needs.

15

Affirming and Blessing Your Son

Shepherding Him into Manhood

Father's Day dawned and we all attended John Kilpatrick's Church of His Presence. Pastor Kilpatrick had pastored the Brownsville Revival and later the Bay of the Holy Spirit Revival.

This morning, however, was Father's Day, and pastor preached a sermon on "The Mystery and Power of the Blessing." I had never heard anything like it.

Then Pastor Kilpatrick invited the fathers to come up for prayer, and it was amazing. He placed his hand on my face, and I thought I would pass out. It felt like rivers of blessing flowing from his hand into me.

I needed that pastor's blessing, since my dad never blessed me. Oh, how I needed it!

Afterward we all headed back to the camp for a final Father's Day Sunday dinner. I could sense that the staff seemed unusually excited. They knew something would be happening after lunch that would be the crowning touch of the whole retreat.

THE BLESSING TUNNEL

After a great Father's Day Dinner, we gathered back in the chapel for our final service. Pastor Ryan, Dr. Sandy, and several other staff members gave their parting words of encouragement and vision. Now it was time for our closing "Blessing Tunnel," where fathers would pray a blessing over their sons.

Pastor Ryan explained, "Our leaders will form two lines, which make up the tunnel. Then the fathers will be invited to make a single-file line and walk slowly through the tunnel of prayer. We will lay hands on you and bless you with the power of the Holy Spirit."

He continued, "Now some of you have never received the fullness of the Spirit. You see, when you got saved, Jesus sent the Holy Spirit to live *in* you; but He wants to come *upon* you, to flood your whole being and give you the power to minister. It's like what happened on the Day of Pentecost in the Bible: "And they were all filled with the Holy Spirit" (Acts 2:4).

As each of us walked slowly through the tunnel, all the leaders prayed over us, and then we became part of the tunnel for our sons.

Pastor Ryan said, "Dads, this is your opportunity to lay hands on your sons and pray a blessing over them, as they walk through the tunnel."

Now it got really messy. Fun but messy. We laid our hands on our sons, praying, "More of You, Jesus!" "More Holy Spirit!" "More hunger for God's Word!" "More joy, more holiness, more love, more passion for souls!" "More grace to forgive!"

The chapel exploded with young men weeping, laughing, and being filled with more of the Holy Spirit. Many of them became so filled they could barely walk. Some simply sat on the floor and quietly wept.

This Blessing Tunnel was like the ultimate experience of the entire healing weekend. It overflowed with love between fathers and sons. If anyone still held a fragment of resentment, it all washed away in this holy river of God's presence. When the Blessing Tunnel ended, the chapel was filled with so much joy that no one wanted to leave.

Shawn and I sat together on the floor, watching the happiness that beamed from each father and son's face. Joy and laughter broke out all through the chapel.

Pastor Ryan said, "This is what Jonathan Edwards called, 'God besotted.' Like those on the day of Pentecost, they were drunk on the goodness of God's new wine (Acts 2:1-12)."

And so ended our last and greatest day of the Father's Day Retreat. We all packed up our cars and said our good-byes. As we turned our car eastward, Shawn and I decided to go the scenic route along the coastline as far as we could. We were excited to talk over everything we had learned and the wonderful ways the Holy Spirit had touched us.

We talked on and on, recounting the great catch of fish at the beach, the joy of sharing in overflowing hearts, the powerful baptisms in the pool, the blessing God poured out on this morning at the church, and of course the "Blessing Tunnel."

Then Shawn said, "You know, Dad, the greatest part for me was getting closer to you and growing closer to the Lord. I keep thinking about the amazing love He showed when He came to save us. Because He came down and drank every drop of the Father's cup, now we can be filled with the Father's Blessing—a cup overflowing with love and salvation."

I looked at my son and marveled. To myself I thought, *I can't get over the depth of maturity I see growing in my son. He's no longer a boy; he's becoming a real man. I wish I knew how to tell him. My dad never told me, but I know I need to be able to guide my son into manhood. I only wish I knew what to say.*

Shawn nodded off to sleep now, leaving me to my own thoughts.

CALLING YOUR SON INTO MANHOOD

Before we continue on to the conclusion of this story, let's consider why it is so important for dads to shepherd their boys into manhood.

John Eldredge, in *Wild at Heart*, wrote, "Every man's deepest fear is to be exposed, to be found out, to be discovered as an imposter, and not really a man."[54]

Gordon Dalbey, the expert on father-wounds agrees:

The father confirms and calls forth masculinity in the son. Without this essential input from Dad, the boy can't later see himself as a man. Quickly, fearfully, the gap between his inadequacy and the man he longs to become fills with a crippling shame.[55]

This is why so many men walk around with a sense of yearning inside. Dalbey says, "I'm convinced that what the men are missing is a sense of their own identity: a very primitive and very deep sense of validation that passes from father to son."[56]

Eldredge tells the story of his young son, Sam, who was rock climbing one day. He hit a snag where a rock jutted out, but in a few more moves he would be at the top. Eldredge encouraged, "Way to go, Sam. You're a *wild man!*" Later, Sam sidled up to his dad and said in a quiet voice, "Dad...did you really think I was a wild man up there?"

Eldredge said, "Miss that moment and you'll miss a boy's heart forever. It's not a question—it's *the* question, the one every boy and man is longing to ask. Do I have what it takes? Am I powerful? Until a man knows he's a man, he will forever be trying to prove he is one, while at the same time shrinking from anything that might reveal he is not. Most men live their lives haunted by the question or crippled by the answer they've been given."[57]

Sometimes an insecure man will try to put on the tough-guy, macho image, refusing to talk about feelings and never shedding a tear.[58] But he's not being real. Dalbey says it simply, "Real men are real."[59]

That's why it is so important for boys to know what it means to be a man. Dr. Bill Bennett, on "James Dobson's Family Talk," said that a real man loves his family; he protects his family; he leads his family, not with dominance but with wisdom and love.[60] Furthermore, he honors his wife and treats her with love; and in turn, she treats him with what he needs most—genuine respect.

TRUE MASCULINITY

In primitive societies, "rites of passage" exist in which the father calls out the manhood in his son. But in our Western culture, this is a forgotten art. Because true manhood is being vilified by so many today, as never before, a son needs his father's masculine input. Boys growing up in this 21st Century are often confused about what it means to be a man.[61]

And though some would try to repudiate masculinity, calling it toxic, actually masculinity comes from God. It means maleness. The Bible says, "Male and female He created them.... and it was very good" (Gen. 1:27, 31, NASB).

Masculinity in God's eyes is "good." Only that which corrupts pure masculinity is toxic, such as aggression, bullying, abuse, violence, and other ungodly qualities. John Eldredge says, "God made the masculine heart, set it within every man, and thereby offers him an invitation: Come, and live out what I meant you to be."[62]

Gordon Dalbey tells a story about Burt Reynolds on the Johnny Carson Show in 1990. Carson asked Reynolds, who was usually cast in strong masculine roles, "What is a real man?" Reynolds replied, "You're not a man 'till your father says you're a man."[63]

Every young man needs to hear his dad say, "Son, I'm proud of you and I respect you. You are becoming a real man." And yet, if a young man never gets this affirmation from his dad or a man he admires, he will carry a father-wound. He may try to prove himself with sexual conquests and physical exploits, but he never really feels like a man unless his father or mentor affirms it.

Indeed, it is this masculine essence, exuding from a father, that slowly, through the years, calls a son into manhood. Like a plant needing water, like a day needing sunshine, a boy needs the masculine contribution of a father. That's what Brad now struggles to try to put into words.

WHAT A SON NEEDS TO HEAR

As we drove along, I thought about the first time I held Shawn as a baby. That first time I held my son to my chest, it was almost like something happened, man-to-man, father-to-son. It seemed like a deep, unspoken masculine root was forming and binding us together.

For a long time, I was lost in thought. I kept thinking of all the things a good father should model for his son. *I know I still need to affirm my son's manhood, but I'm not sure what to say. My own father never affirmed me, so I don't know how to give what I never received.*

Finally, Shawn, opened his eyes and stretched. After a little small talk, I said, "Son, you know, I've been thinking about how I can be a better father. I need you to help me with that."

We drove in silence for most of the way home, lost in thought and still basking in the wonder of the weekend. At last after several hours of driving, I turned into our driveway and stopped the car.

Shawn started to open the door, but I reached over and put my hand on his shoulder. "Wait, Son, there's something important I need to tell you…"

He looked at me, puzzled.

"You know I've been amazed at your spiritual growth over the last few months, especially the maturity you showed when you forgave me on the beach. And when you gave your testimony in the chapel at the camp, I saw such depth of wisdom. You've proven something to me that I've longed to see."

With fatherly love welling up within me, I looked him in the eyes and said, "Son, I want you to know I'm very proud of you. I really respect your growth, your manly maturity, and the godly wisdom

I've seen in you. You are becoming a *real man!* Even more, you are becoming a *real man of God!*"

Shawn took in a deep breath and smiled broadly. "Thanks, Dad, that means everything to me." No greater words could ever be spoken from a father to his son.

Shawn started to open the car door, but I stopped him again. "There's one more thing, Son."

I swallowed and took a deep breath, gathering my courage. "This is hard for me because I'm new to this stuff, but I want to give you something I never had. I want to give you a Father's Blessing."

A look of awe and appreciation came over Shawn. He reverently bowed his head. I laid my hand on his head and prayed:

> *Father, I don't know how to do this, but I want to give my son what my own dad never gave me. I bless you, Shawn, with my love and the love of God. I bless your future career. I bless your future wife. I bless your children and my grandchildren. Jesus, I pray that my son, Shawn, will be the man of God you have called him to be and he will honor You all the days of his life. Amen.*

Shawn looked up at me, his eyes wet but shining. "Thank you, Dad. I will always remember this blessing. This has been powerful!"

He thought for another moment and said, "And I will always remember this weekend. It has been the greatest time of my life!"

"Me too, Son. Me too."

"Hey," blurted Shawn as he opened the car door, "Let's go tell Mom. She will be ecstatic!"

FIVE STEPS FOR REACHING YOUR SON'S HEART

Let's look once more at a recap of the Five steps for *Reaching Your Son's Heart.*

1. Open your wound to the light and let God cleanse and heal your own infected father-wound. He will wash away the grief and cleanse away the bitterness until you are fully able to forgive your own dad.

2. Forgive yourself completely, and then, humbly and sincerely, ask your son's forgiveness.

3. To soften his heart and help him fully forgive you, tell him your own father-wound story.

4. Wait for the right time, and then affirm your son as a man. But don't stop there. Keep on affirming his masculine, godly qualities for the rest of his life. He still needs it from his dad.

5. Give your son the power of "The Father's Blessing." This will affect him, his wife and children, and his children's children all their lives.

These five steps can be worked through on your own with the Lord, but it will help if you come to our retreat or have someone who will read through this book and stand in the gap for your father, repenting to you and praying with you.

Now, as we come to our last chapter, we will fast forward five years from now to experience a precious miracle in Bradley Hudson's life.

16

The Most Beautiful Sound in the World

Reaching the Heart of Your Dad

"Hurry, Brad! Hurry! It's almost time," cried Megan.

"I'm going as fast as I can without having a wreck. I'm as excited as you are! C'mon, let's just pray," I said, trying to appear calm, but in reality, my hands shook and tears blinded my eyes so badly I could hardly see the road.

"Yes, Yes, Oh, God please help us get there safely and just in time!" Megan cried.

"And Father," I broke in, "Keep your hand on our kids. Help Shawn to be the man he needs to be during this mountain peak in his life. Help him support his wife, Gracey, during this crucial time."

"Please, God, no prolapse or umbilical cord around the baby's neck! This is our *grandbaby!* Please let this birth go smoothly, not like what Brad and I experienced 25 years ago."

"Lord, we thank You for turning our lives around through the years. You have blessed our family like we could never have dreamed. And now we ask you to bless Shawn and Gracey in that hospital room."

A sudden memory flashed before me, and I turned to Megan. "Honey, I remember the time, five years ago, when Shawn and I had just returned home from the retreat. Before we got out of the car, I laid my hand on Shawn's head and gave him *The Father's Blessing*. This was all so new to me, and I didn't know what I was doing, but I was earnestly sincere."

"I can see that memory of Shawn and me sitting in the car like it was yesterday. My whole heart was in that prayer as I prayed that God would pour his blessing out upon Shawn's life and would make him a man of God. Then I prayed for his future wife and his children and his grandchildren."

"Oh, Brad, I'm so thankful you did that. It's so good for a father to give his children this blessing."

"Yes, and Shawn took it very seriously. But now I'm thinking that these kids are still under this blessing. I believe God will be with them as they bring our grandson into the world!"

"I wonder what they will name him?" Megan added. "Have they hinted to you at all?"

"No, not a word. For some reason they want to keep this a secret. We sure weren't that way, were we, Honey? We wanted everyone to know our son would be called Shawn Michael Hudson!"

"Oh, well, we have to let them lead their own lives and not interfere too much," Megan said wisely.

"I wish this hospital were not so far away," I moaned.

"There it is! I can see the lights of the hospital just up ahead!" Megan squealed.

I parked the car and we rushed into the entrance, searching out the elevator to the maternity ward. I squeezed Meg's hand so tightly, she winced. *I think the longest ride on earth is an elevator to a maternity ward!*

After what seemed like an eternal wait, the doors slid open, and we dashed down the hall. Megan headed straight for the nurse's station, telling them who we are and asking if we could we go in to see what is happening?

A kindly older nurse said, "Let me check."

She entered a room and came back shortly. Just behind her came Shawn. He seemed overjoyed to see us. This was such a high point in his life, but he had never been through this before, and he needed his mom and dad.

He hugged us both and gushed, "The baby is almost here! I feel like I'm about to faint with fear and excitement."

"Hold on, Son. This will be fine. God is with you and we will be out here praying."

Shawn hurried back to be with Gracey, and Meg and I sat down in the waiting room. A few other people were there, but we joined hands anyway and quietly prayed. We waited, it seemed like, forever.

Finally, Shawn peeked his head out and gave us a thumbs up. "The baby is coming!" he beamed.

"Brad, that was the very point when the doctor suddenly shouted 'Prolapse!'" Megan groaned. "Dear God, please keep our grandbaby safe..."

We were half praying, half listening, holding our breath. Then suddenly, we heard it—the wild wailing cry of a newborn baby!

It seemed to us like the most beautiful sound in the whole world. The cry was full and rich and clear.

We both remembered vividly how our son couldn't breathe at his birth. In spite of my terror I had laid a trembling hand on his little chest and, as his father, commanded him to breathe. Suddenly, he let out that same beautiful, wild, wailing scream—oh, the cry of a newborn baby!

We jumped up, ran to the door, and peeked in. Shawn looked up and saw us. He smiled broadly and motioned for us to come on in. We were elated.

The residents were cleaning up the baby as we entered. Shawn was wiping Gracey's brow from perspiration. He jumped up and hugged us, crying and laughing with joy.

The resident nurse handed the baby to his daddy as they cleaned up Gracey, preparing her to nurse.

Brad watched Shawn sit down in a chair, holding his baby closely. He knew just how he felt. Shawn could almost feel the baby's heartbeat as he held him next to his chest. He snuggled him in even closer, nestling him over his shoulder. He closed his eyes as he seemed to be absorbing the sweetness of his son.

Soon the resident reached for the baby and laid him across his mother. The nurse coaxed Gracey and the baby to nurse. And Megan looked on, adjusting pillows and helping burp the baby as needed.

As the women attended to mom and baby, Shawn stood and walked over to me. The look on his face betrayed the emotion on his mind.

He hugged me tightly and whispered in my ear, "I hope I can be as good a dad as you have been!"

"What? Me!" His words washed over me like a warm ocean wave. I could hardly believe he would say such a thing. I hung my head and said, "Well, we had some pretty tough years there, but the Lord has brought us through.... I'm so proud of you, Son."

Shawn said, "Dad, I have something for you." He motioned me over to the corner of the room. Then he handed me a little box.

"First, I want to say a few things to you, Dad." Everyone in the room quieted down and listened.

"I want to thank you for being such a great dad!"

I feel honestly embarrassed because I'm so undeserving of these kind words, but he just kept on battering my heart with gratitude. I could hardly bear it.

"Thank you for believing in me when I didn't believe in myself. Thank you for reaching out to me even when I would spit in your face. Thank you for never giving up on me and for forgiving me for all the pain I brought you."

"Thank you for stepping down a few notches from the ladder on your job, so we could spend more time together. Thank you for loving me through the turbulent teenage years. Thank you for humbling yourself and repenting to me and asking my forgiveness. Thank you for being vulnerable and opening your heart to tell me your painful story."

"Thank you for sincerely affirming me as a man and for giving me your heartfelt father's blessing. Thank you for being my dad."

My heart swelled and I could hardly contain myself. It seemed as though all the grief and suffering of my whole life had all washed away through the blood of Christ and now the affirmation of my son.

At last, it seemed as though a new day of loving my family and loving my God had dawned upon my life. I stood there blushing and trembling and mopping my tears, trying to take it all in. Megan was also dabbing at her tears.

"Oh and Dad, Gracey and I have a little gift we want to give you."

I opened my hand to receive the little box and then I nervously tried to unwrap it. Finally, I tore away the paper and opened the box. Nestled amidst the blue tissue paper was a little bronze baby shoe with a brass plate beneath it.

Shawn's eyes twinkled as he explained. "This is a baby shoe, but it has our baby's name written on the plate. We wanted you and mom to be the first to know..."

I looked at the plate through my tears. Engraved into the brass was our grandson's name:

Bradley J. Hudson

"Ohhh..." gasped Brad, breathless and stunned, overwhelmed by surprise and the honor of this tribute.

"Now, Dad, before you start bawling, I want to introduce you to your grandson." Megan had been resting him over her shoulder so she could be ready at the proper time. She walked over to me and laid the baby into my arms.

With glistening eyes, she said, "Say Hello to your namesake, Bradley J. Hudson!" I had the feeling she already knew all about this.

I reached out and held him, enthralled. I closed my eyes and cuddled him close. I felt like I would never let him go.

The room filled with quiet emotion. Moments passed and Megan held up another box, wrapped in pale blue paper and garnished with a royal blue bow. "Don't forget our gift to them," she reminded.

"Oh, yes," whispered Brad, with Baby Bradley still asleep on his shoulder. "I picked this out myself."

Shawn opened the gift and burst into tears.

Inside the box, filled with white tissue paper, was a man's baseball glove with a little boy's glove and ball.

No words were needed. This said it all.

THE HEARTS OF CHILDREN TO FATHERS

I'm sure you can see how this story has come full circle. From a father who wounds his son to a son who honors his father.

Now I want to ask you—what if all over this wounded nation, young men and women started reaching out, like Shawn, expressing forgiveness, love, and honor to their dads? This book gives steps for reaching your son's wounded heart, but what if you took steps for reaching your dad's wounded heart?

What if you really forgave your dad for his mistakes, even if he's never asked your forgiveness? What if you even stooped to wash his feet?

What if you asked your dad to tell you his story of pain, asking him what hurt him the most? Then what if you stood in for his dad and repented to him for his worst and most painful memories.

What if you did what Nick did in his story at the retreat in Chapter 8. What if you placed your hands on his shoulders, looked straight into his eyes, and said, "I forgive you, Dad. No matter what has happened between us, I love you unconditionally because you are my dad and I am your son, nothing will ever change that fact."

What if you prayed with him, even though he may not believe? What if you prayed, asking Jesus to wash away all the past hurt and pain between you? What if you prayed and invoked the power of the blood, the power of the cross, and the power of the name of Jesus?

What if this would open the door of his heart to Jesus, like with Nick and his dad? What if you were now able to reach out and lead your dad to receive the Lord? Can you see the massive healing this would bring between you? It would wash away his guilt and shame and enable him to look you in the eye once again.

I wrote this book for dads to encourage them to reach out to you. Now I'm asking you to reach out to your dad. What if we all did that? It would change the world!

GOD'S BLESSING ON THE EARTH

I finished this book during the throes of the Corona Virus in 2020. As this curse of a pandemic, killing hundreds of thousands, has swept our planet, I believe this is a watershed moment for all of us. What do you think would happen if children everywhere began reaching out to their fathers, and fathers everywhere began reaching out to their children.

The Old Testament ends with an astounding verse: "He will restore the hearts of the fathers to their children and the hearts of the children to their fathers, so that I will not come and smite the land with a curse" (Mal. 4:6).

But what do you think would happen if we did indeed see fathers reaching out to their children and children reaching out to their dads? If we could all make this colossal effort to reach out to one another, think what this could bring. Not a "curse" on the land, but a great national healing in America's wounded children and their dads.

And maybe this would be one more way our world can be healed. If at last, our fathers and children are restored, I believe God would pour down upon the land, not a curse, but a blessing beyond measure—a massive harvest of souls, world-wide revival like this earth has never known, and a Third Great Awakening!

Lift Him Back to Your Heart

A Final Call to Fathers

Before you lay this book aside, I want to finish a story I started telling you earlier. It's about the time my dad took me, as a little baby, into the churning Atlantic waters. It was during a hurricane warning, and suddenly a massive wave washed me right out of his arms. He thrashed through the turbulence until, at last, he touched a little hand. He grabbed me and pulled me out of the deep, holding me tightly.

Now I want to finish the story by telling you what happened 46 years later, when I reached out and took my father's hand, lifting him out of dark waters as well.

One day I received a call from my mother saying, "Daddy is dying and if you hurry you might get here before it's too late." I quickly got my kids out of school and rushed to the hospital three hours away in Abilene, Texas. When I arrived, I hurried into ICU where my dad was in a coma.

My younger sister, Debbie said, "Sandy, help him! He's a good man. He deserves to go to heaven!"[64]

It's true, he was a wonderful man, but my parents were atheists, and I knew his good works couldn't get him into heaven.

Now, here was my sister crying, "Help him, Sandy! He deserves to go to heaven!"

But he's in a coma, I thought. *What could I do? It's too late! Oh, well, I'll try anyway...* I reached out a quavering hand and clasped his hand. "Daddy, do you want to go to heaven and be with Jesus?"

To my utter shock, he groaned, "Uh huh!" I gasped and looked at Debbie. *Am I hearing things?* I wondered. *Did that really just happen?* I wasn't sure so I said again, "Daddy, do you want to be with Jesus and go to heaven?"

"Uh huh!" he said again. My heart leapt to my throat. I tightened my grip on his hand. I took a deep breath and said, "I know you can't speak, but, Daddy, I'm going to lead you in a prayer to receive the Lord. Say these words in your heart." I prayed out loud with him and led him through a prayer to ask forgiveness and to receive Christ.

Suddenly, Debbie cried, "Look!" I looked, and there—rolling down his cheek—was a huge tear. That tear spoke volumes. It told me that something had happened in his heart.

And though he was expected to die within moments, he came out of the coma and lived for three more weeks. Every time I saw him, he wanted to pray or talk about the Lord. He was a changed man.

I look back now and realize—decades ago, my father reached out a hand and lifted me back into his arms. Now I reached out my hand and helped lift him into the arms of God.

As I've said, I see this story as a metaphor for our times. Our young men have been drowning in a cultural sea of confusion. As little boys, they are told, "big boys don't cry." Then as they step into their teen years, many of them carry an aching father-wound pulsing deep in their souls. If they repress the grief and anger, this may result in depression and suicide, or even crime and violence.

Our young men need caring fathers who will reach out, take them by the hand, then lift them back to their hearts, and ultimately back to the heart of God.

IT'S NEVER TOO LATE

America's Coach, Joe Ehrmann, said "If you were on your deathbed, you would ask yourself, What kind of father was I? What kind of husband? What kind of son?"[65]

Do these questions strike a nerve of regret? If so, I want to tell you—it is not too late.

You may feel like you botched it as a dad, but you did not stop being a father when your son or daughter moved out. You may no longer be married to their mother, but you are still their dad.

Even if you are old and near the end of your life, it's still not too late. You are not on your death bed, and you have the rest of your life to get it right and to be a great father. As long as you are still breathing, it is not too late!

I told you in the beginning that this book is not religious. It is not. But it is spiritual, for it deals with issues of the heart. And only Jesus has the power to heal a human heart. Now I want Bradley Hudson to be the one to give us a final word of wisdom.

BRADLEY HUDSON'S LAST WORD

I opened my story by telling you, "My ambition to climb the corporate ladder came to a screeching halt when I raised my garage door and found my son hanging from a rope."

Today, as a grandfather, I've learned a few things. I believe God looked down and saw all of us scaling our own ladders—ladders of success, fame, fortune, popularity, position, good works—you name it.

In the midst of our climb, He disrupted our lives with something we never would have imagined.

He opened His heart and sent down His only Son to hang—not from a rope but from a cross. Not from a noose but from three nails. Now He reaches out a nail-pierced hand to you and whispers—"*Live, Son, live!*"

Acknowledgements

When I think of the ones who have influenced the writing of this book, I think first of Steve Harrison of Bradley Communications. Steve helped me with more than writing. He helped me reach down into my heart and pull out the message that burns most deeply. He encouraged me to reveal the primary reason why so many young adults and teens have received healing for father-wounds at our camp.

Secondly, I think of Martha Bullen. Everybody loves Martha because she helps us so much in writing books. She helped me wrestle over book titles and book covers and she skillfully guided me through the publishing and launching process.

I also think about my appreciation for Geoffrey Berwind, a wonderfully talented man who works for Bradley Communications. Geoffrey helped hone my message and showed me the great value of storytelling.

Then I think of those who have given me priceless feedback, like Brandon, Scarlet, Ashley, Laura, my daughters Misti and Christi, Guy and Lenora, Ryan and Thomas and many others. LaDonna, a respiratory therapist, especially helped me with medical issues and feedback in the book.

I also think of my Pastor John Kilpatrick who pastored the Bay of the Holy Spirit Revival and the Brownsville Revival as well as

Church of His Presence in Daphne, Alabama. He has mentored me in revival and taught me many things. He especially taught me about the power of the father's blessing. He has encouraged and inspired me through the last twenty years.

I must also mention Dr. James Dobson who has tirelessly worked to shepherd America's families through decades of tumultuous times. His Internet radio program, "Dr James Dobson's Family Talk" has had a huge impact on my life, and his book *Bringing Up Boys* has helped shape this book for *Reaching Your Wounded Son*.

And of course, most of all I acknowledge my Lord and Savior Jesus Christ for paying the ultimate price. He deserves our deepest gratitude, for He shed His blood to cleanse us from sin and heal our bleeding wounds. He was broken so that we could reach our broken boys.

APPENDIX

An Invitation for Fathers and Sons

THE FATHER'S DAY RETREAT

Date: One week after Father's Day, June 24-28, 2021

(Held Yearly on Father's Day, after 2021)

Camp America Ablaze for The Lamb

12251 County Rd. 91, Lillian, Al 36549

I want to invite you to attend our annual Father's Day Retreat on the Gulf Coast of Alabama. This is the retreat you read about in this book. It will give you an opportunity to hang out with your son for 4–5 days of fun, relationship building, healing, and inspiration.

You'll visit the gleaming white sands of our beautiful beach, play volleyball, tennis, basketball or softball at the camp. You'll roast hotdogs around the campfire, you'll be inspired by stories of other fathers and sons, and your father-wounds will be healed..

We expect this retreat to become an annual event, bringing fathers and sons (of all ages) together. As you reconnect with your son, the bond between you will tighten. You will put into practice the principles you've learned in this book. This will affect your family for generations to come, for you will be restored to the heart of your son.

To register or learn more about this retreat
and other events, visit our website
www.beholdthelamb.org or
www.reachingyoursonsheart.org

How I Got My Son Back!

A Father's Story of His Son's Healing
BY RUBEN TORRES
(businessman)

I grew up in Venezuela, but when I moved to America and became a husband and a father, I always knew I needed to provide well for my family. My father, a general in the Air Force, instilled this in me. He also taught me to be the very best at whatever I did.

I joined the military, though I thought I never would. I became a respected and somewhat decorated infantryman in the U.S Army. I was promoted ahead of my peers, and I had very prestigious assignments because I was driven to be the best.

Naturally I had become successful (superficially), but I was actually empty and broken inside. I lacked purpose in my life, but I could not see it for myself. I had a beautiful wife and the most amazing children anyone could ask for. The values of humility, respect, and honor had passed to my children and I did not even realize it.

After the military, I began a successful career in distribution. I enjoyed it and learned it very quickly. With success, came promotions into new distribution centers in new cities and states.

We moved every 18 months for many years. My wife and children humbly followed my journey and supported all these moves. My daughter attended 11 different schools by the time she graduated high school. One of my greatest regrets is that I did not notice what these moves and school relocations were doing to my precious children.

Then one night, while living in a temporary apartment, my son attempted suicide. This was the saddest and scariest moment in my life. My beautiful and humble boy did not think life was worth living. This gripped my spirit and my life became filled with an overwhelming love and passion for my family.

You see, what I haven't mentioned yet is that I encountered Jesus like never before just a few months before my son tried to take his own life. My son, Adrian, and I attended a Behold the Lamb internship in Lillian, Alabama in the spring of 2014. My niece had attended this internship and told us about this incredible encounter she had with Jesus. I was saved and had been living, actually striving, to do God's will. I did not understand God's promises or Jesus' sacrifice, and was living in shame and regret.

When we first entered onto the grounds of this camp in Lillian, it was like we entered into heaven. I saw and felt Jesus' presence and did not even know what it was. My son, who was very shy and introspective then, smiled for the first time in many months. We did not know what was happening, but neither of us wanted it to end. We met the cross and the cup Jesus drank for us for the first time.

When you first see Jesus' face and the punishment he took in our place when He drank the Father's cup at Calvary, you finally understand what we mean to him. You finally grasp the level of love the Father has for us. You finally see the incredible sacrifice that both the Son and the Father made for me and for you.

The shame, regret, and condemnation that I lived with for all those years was suddenly lifted off my life. It was the most amazing and incredible feeling of love and everlasting freedom I've ever experienced.

My entire life, and even my life after salvation had been filled with regret and shame. I was ashamed of who I was and what I had done. Even after accepting Jesus as my Lord and Savior, I was living in condemnation. It was only after I met Jesus face to face during that internship that I understood the Love that we have. Jesus, as the Lamb of God, offered himself as a living sacrifice. He took our punishment so we may live free!

Even after finding Jesus at this camp, I didn't realize how much my son was hurting. But all this time, he had been missing his father, and I was too busy "providing" for him to love him. Every son deserves a father, and as a father I was failing him.

That sad evening, I received a call from my son's cell phone. He and my daughter were sleeping in the bedroom downstairs, and my wife and I were in the bedroom upstairs. This was a temporary apartment that was provided for us during this work assignment. My son told me: "dad, please come down." His voice was unusually worried, and I trembled inside.

I ran down as fast as I could run and went into his room. He told me: "I need to go to the hospital." I started to walk with him to the car while I asked him what had happened. He then told me what no father ever wants to hear—"I took some pills!"

At that very moment, my world crumbled. My boy had become so depressed that he attempted to take his own life. I felt broken in ways I can't explain. As we were walking out of the room, my wife and daughter joined us. We rushed to the hospital, and we walked with him directly to the back of the emergency room.

It was very late at night, so there wasn't anyone else there. I don't think I would have noticed anyone either way. The doctors saw him immediately and told us that they needed to evaluate him physically first. Once he was okay physically, they said that he was going to see a psychologist for evaluation.

I could not grasp the reality of this. Why did he do this? What did I do to create this? What should I have done differently? All these questions were flowing through my head, and I did not have any answers. You see, as the head of a family, a man must have answers. This is what I thought: the man must respond, provide, resolve and protect his family. I did not do any of this, and my son was suffering because of me.

As my son was laying on the hospital bed after he woke up, I looked him in the eye and told him that I loved him. I told him that I was sorry, and I told him that God's plans for his life were tremendous. This was not full repentance, but I was trying to comfort him.

At this point, I did not know why, but I knew that it was my fault. After my son was evaluated by the psychologist, he was referred to a different facility for further evaluation and counseling. He was taken to a psychological treatment facility. My wife and I followed the ambulance and walked with him through every chilling step of this admission.

This was a cold and quiet facility. All I could ask the staff was, "When can my son come home?" Of course, no one could give me an answer. Finally, he was admitted to a young adult area, and the staff there re-assured us of his time there. They told us that it was too late that night, and that the doctor will speak to us the next day. We left and came back as soon as they allowed us the next morning.

The diagnosis was that my son was "clinically depressed." The doctor explained to us that the repeated moves, the up-coming move, his friends and the lack of stability had depressed him. I cannot put into words the shame, regret and guilt that overwhelmed me. I never blamed anyone for this. It was my fault. My wife and I prayed without ceasing and we had faith that God will deliver his promises to us. Our son would be delivered from this.

During this time, we called Dr. Sandy, who hosted the internship Adrian and I attended. She right away jumped in with endless faith and prayer for our son. She comforted us and gave us hope. Jesus was there, and he was going to deliver my family from this overwhelming pain. I knew that my son was going to be okay regardless of the current circumstances. After 2 days and several counseling sessions, my son was finally released. He was very quiet about the whole experience.

After we had a chance to sit down and talk, I repented to him and told him I was sorry about the repeated moves, about my lack as a father, and about the difficult circumstances we had at home. I promised him that once we moved to a permanent home, since the current living circumstance was temporary, he would attend a great high school for the entire high school period. I assured him that

God was going to open for us a wonderful school where he could make new friends and enjoy these important years. I promised him that we would not move again during his high school years.

I was very sorry, and I wanted him to know it. I wanted him to believe that God's promises were true, and that our circumstances would get better. I also wanted him to believe that I loved him. However, I needed actions and not just words. Since that moment, I have prayed every day for my son to have God's anointing in his life and for God to keep him in the shadow of his wings (Psalms 91).

My wife and I pray without ceasing for our children, and for their lives. The following months were critical. I wanted to be the man God created me to be, and not the provider I thought I needed to be. After this terrible ordeal, my wife suggested to Adrian that he come back to the camp. This is when he had a total transformation, but I'll let him tell you that part of his story…

Meanwhile, during our time at the camp, Adrian had been prophesied over and God spoke great words upon his life. This prophesy has since come to pass in a lot of ways. During this difficult trial, this prophesy seemed so distant and unreal. The Holy Spirit, through a prophet, told my son that he would preach the Gospel to multitudes, and that many would be saved. He would plant churches that would help save multitudes, and as these churches begin to grow, God will call him to his next assignment. Of all the wonderful things we lived in this camp, this prophesy has been an unwavering truth.

Although at one point, this seemed so distant, God has worked in my son's life in supernatural ways. No matter how much I can provide for my son—clothes, food, housing, school, or any other physical need, I was not providing the love and nurturing a father needs to give. I was not showing him how to love and live in communion with the Father, the Son and the Holy Spirit. I feel blessed to have my boy back, and to have a second chance to provide our true duty in this life – to be a father.

Four years later, my son is now a senior in High School with high hopes and dreams after graduation. He is on staff at the camp we attended, and he wants to pursue a college career in a Christian University and Ministry School. He is also a very passionate preacher and evangelist. He has taken the Gospel to many distant places in the country, and even into Europe through a mission trip.

In high school, he has planted life groups where he pours his heart out to young people struggling to find truth. He regularly preaches at school functions where he helps bring many young people to Christ. He has become a mentor of many young and old. He has been invited to speak at many conferences, retreats, and evangelist missions. My son has become a great evangelist with a passion for young people. His wisdom and experience are so much greater than his years. I am so proud of him, and I thank God for hearing the cry of my heart. He has restored our relationship and shown me how to be a real father. Like this book says, I have discovered that it's never too late to get your broken boy back!

How My Mess Became A Message

A Son's Story of Forgiveness and Restoration

BY ADRIAN TORRES

I was broken. Nobody knew how lonely I felt. My dad was in the military, and we had to move over and over again. Just when I had finally made new friends, we had to move again. My life seemed hopeless. We had moved from California to Georgia, and I never felt welcome anywhere.

To make matters worse, my parents were about to split up. My mom kept saying she wanted to leave everything and move across the country. She always offered to take me with her but I never wanted to leave my friends. Then my dad got called to a new job so he moved up to the northeast while my sister and I stayed back with my mom.

That's when our house caught fire and burned down. I felt completely homeless. We didn't even have a real home. I didn't know God so my heart was empty, and we didn't even have each other as a family.

My mom decided it was too hard to take care of everything by herself. She ripped me out of school and we moved to be with my dad. Here in New Jersey we lived in two separate apartments, but I stayed home most of the time and locked myself in my room. I spent hours listening to heavy-metal music, playing video games, and watching horror movies. This dark stuff seemed to feed the hatred that was seething inside me, especially for my dad.

During that time, I came to Dr. Sandy's camp in Alabama. I planned to run away when I got there, but my dad came with me, so I couldn't get away. Finally, the Lord broke through to my heart, but I didn't know how to hold on to my faith. My dad really got close to God, but I lost it when I got home.

Now my parents told me we were moving again. That was it! I knew I wouldn't go. I just couldn't take anymore. I was hurting so badly, so one night I overdosed on drugs. It was late at night, but I called my dad from my cell phone and asked him to come help me. I knew I was dying. My parents were frantic. They rushed me to the Emergency Room at the hospital.

All the way to the hospital, they kept yelling at me. I kept hoping they would at least say, "I love you, Son." But no, they just kept shouting and telling me how stupid I was for taking all those pills. The doctors were shocked that I didn't die. I didn't even have any liver or kidney damage.

After that, we moved to California, and I didn't care about anything. I started drinking, and I had a girlfriend and just cared about getting laid. I was a mess.

Out of the blue one day my mom suggested that I go back to the camp, but I had already decided that all that stuff was not real. I had started going back to church, but I never heard anything about the cross. I finally decided to go to the camp.

When I walked on the grounds, I could feel something different. I was a few days late, but I still felt so at home. At first, Dr. Sandy didn't recognize me because I had grown a lot in two years. But when she hugged me and welcomed me back, I felt so loved.

Soon, I had given my life back to God and I could feel a new fire burning inside me. It was the fire of the cross. One day I started admitting to my brothers about all the horror movies and heavy-metal music I listened to. They prayed for me and I know something left me. It was like a deep haunting darkness came out.

I forgave my dad for all the times we had moved, and when I got home, he repented sincerely to me. I burned all my old videos and music, and I began talking to everyone about Jesus. I started several Bible clubs in my school and they just kept growing.

One day, I heard the heartbreaking news that my good friend, Colton Davis, had been shot. We were friends from football, and how many of you know that football is like a brotherhood. I kept thinking about the fact that I would never see him again.

But even more, I knew he wasn't a Christian and I wished so much that he could have gone to one of my Bible clubs. Then I found out that he didn't just get shot, but he shot himself! That hurt me so much. I kept saying, "Oh, God, if only I could have said something to him about the Lord."

Since then I've been doing my best to lead people to Jesus. Some people tell me I just witness because I have a calling on my life. No!

We are all called to share Christ. We aren't promised tomorrow. We have to share Him while we can. We have to become rivers. Rivers! We can't have any more Coltons die without Christ!

Now I know that if God can take a small, shy kid like me and use me, He can use anyone. And now, I can honestly say—my mess has become a message.

A Father Asks Forgiveness

The following is a list of ways to repent to others for their father-wounds. Let this serve as a guide for how to ask forgiveness of your own son:

Please picture now the face of your dad, saying these words to you. Let them go in deep. This may help unearth some hidden pain and areas of grief and resentment. To clean out these wounds will be life changing for you. So here we go.

- I want to tell you how sorry I am that I impregnated your mom before we were married. I'm sure this brought you shame, and it was wrong. If anyone bullied you or called you "bastard," I am deeply sorry. It was not your fault, and you should never have had to be ashamed.

- I am so sorry that I abandoned you at such a young age. I left your mother and you, and I know this made you feel lonely and lost without a dad.

- I apologize to you for all the drinking and cursing and angry language I used. It was wrong.

- I'm sorry for the way I slapped your mom, beat her, and frightened you. I'm sure you were afraid I would hurt her badly, and if you had been big enough you would have protected her from me.

+   I repent to you for beating and abusing you too. I must have wounded your manhood with my abusive language and critical comments. You were too young to fight me back, and this must have caused deep anger to build inside. I am so sorry for that, Son. It was wrong.

+   I'm sorry for the divorce and for leaving you in such poverty. Your mom had to work and this left you alone and abandoned. I know you must have felt embarrassed for not having the money to do what other kids did. You couldn't afford the name brand shoes and the trendy clothes. I wish I could have given you more, but I'm asking you to please forgive me for the way I let you down.

+   I apologize to you that I got so hooked on pornography and made you feel uncomfortable about what I was doing. I apologize for the other women or men and the way you felt so repulsed by my behavior.

+   I repent to you for not protecting you and your mom and for not making you feel safe and secure.

+   I repent for the way I expected you to live up to my expectations, and I criticized you if you didn't. Please forgive me for not respecting you and giving you space to be who you are.

+   I'm so sorry for all the programs I missed or the ballgames and sports I never attended. Other dads were there, but I was not, and I am so sorry. It was wrong.

+ I'm so sorry I broke my promises and hardly ever kept my word.

+ I'm sorry I spent so little time with you. I rarely if ever hugged you, and I never told you I loved you. That was terribly wrong.

+ I'm sorry I never taught you how to treat a woman. I never knew how to treat women myself so I didn't know how to teach you. I didn't talk to you about sex because I didn't know how to discuss it in a clean way.

+ I apologize for all the birthdays I overlooked. I didn't really forget. It just brought up too much pain to acknowledge, but I was only thinking of how I felt, not how you felt.

+ I am so sorry for the way I tore you down with my words and never encouraged you. I did to you what my dad did to me, and I was wrong. Please forgive me, Son. I let you down in so many ways as a dad.

+ I regret that I embarrassed you in front of your friends. I never affirmed you and I never affirmed your masculinity, I only mocked your weaknesses, as though that would push you to improve. It was wrong.

+ I have wounded you with my own woundedness. I did not model what a godly man is like. I didn't take you to church and pray with you and bless you. But now, God has changed my life. I am asking you to forgive me, and I would like now to speak a Father's Blessing over your life.

How to Give a Father's Blessing

I want to impart to you now a Father's Blessing. As you read this, please try to picture your own dad saying these words, even if he rejected you.

I bless you, my Son, with the blessing that only a father can give. I bless you as part of the masculine heritage of our family line. You are my man-child, my son, and I am very proud of you.

I bless you to grow and have integrity and honesty. I bless you to be a man of truthfulness and reliability. I bless you to always be a man of your word.

I bless you to be a man of morality and godly principles.

I bless you to prosper as your soul prospers.

I bless you to be authentic and real and to speak what you believe.

I bless you to be kind and generous to the poor. I bless you to be considerate of others and to have compassion for broken people.

I bless you as a man who is confident in your manhood, who can embrace your masculinity and live a manly life of purity, without toxic abuse of others.

I bless you to know that I believe in you. You are becoming a man, and I am so proud of you. I pray that no matter where you are or who you are with, you will always know that I believe in you.

I bless every cell of your body to have health and vitality and healing from God when you need it.

I believe in your ability to make good decisions and to stay out of trouble. I bless you to follow after righteousness and goodness.

I bless you to become a fearless and courageous man, confident of who you are in Christ.

I bless you to provide safety and security for the women in your life. To honor and respect women and never to take advantage of a woman. I bless you to remain faithful to one woman, your wife and the mother of your children.

I bless you to become a great father. To be a provider and protector of your family and to always show them the way to God, which is through His Son.

BOOKS BY DR. SANDY

Pierced to the Heart: A Cry to Bring Back the Pure Gospel (launches in June, 2020)

Undone by a Revelation of the Lamb (additional workbook and DVDs)

The Father's Cup (additional Audio book)

Unquenchable Flame (English or German or Spanish)

The Glory of the Lamb

Dad, Where Are You?: How to Heal the Father-wound that Holds You Under (English or Spanish)

Healing the Wounded Heart

Rivers of Glory

The Masterpiece (English or Spanish)

A Revelation of the Lamb for America

America Ablaze

India Ablaze (English, Talagu, Tamil, Malayalim, or Hindi)

The Pain (booklet)

The Pain in an African Heart (booklet)

The Mystery of Avraham's Lamb (also the Audio book)

Bethlehem's Lamb (Second Addition on Kindle)

The Wounded Soldier (also *The Wounded Soldier* Audio book)

Behold and Be Healed (launch date tba)

"Revivalists of the Cross" (*Glory of the Lamb*) DVD SERIES

Wiping the Tears on the Soul of America (Healing Racial Wounds)

Mama Hazel's Genuine Faith

CHILDREN'S BOOKS:

Would Jesus Eat His Vegetables?

How Would Jesus Act at Bedtime?

Would Jesus be a Bad Sport?

To order, visit us online:
www.beholdthelamb.org
or Amazon.com

Retreats, Camps, and Internships

Summer: "Behold the Lamb"
Families, Teens, Young Adults Camp. (2 wks in July)

Fall: "Daughters of Revival"

Spring: "Behold the Lamb" Retreat in April

Summer, June 2021: Father and Son Retreat
Experience a time of fun, fellowship, and inspiration and
healing of father-wounds with your son or grandson.

Camp America Ablaze
12251 C Rd. 91, Lillian, AL 36549

For more information visit our website:
www.beholdthelamb.org
www.AmericasBrokenBoys or
www.reachingyoursonsheart.com

Endnotes

Introduction: Longing to be Restored to Your Son

1   Gordon Dalbey, *Father and Son* (Nashville: Thomas Nelson Publishers,1992), p. 5.

2   James Dobson, Bringing Up Boys: Practical Advice and Encouragement for Those Shaping the Next Generation of Men (Carol Stream, IL: Tyndale House Publishers, Tyndale Momentum, 2001), p. 33.

PART I: THE STORY OF A FATHER AND SON

Chapter One: Climbing the Ladder to Nowhere (no notes)

Chapter Two: The Bond Between a Father and His Son

3   Gordon Dalbey, *Sons of the Father: Healing the Father-Wound in Men* (Folsom, CA: Civitas Press, 2011), p. 10.

4   Stephen Strange, *Old Man, New Man* (Lake Mary, FL: Creation House, 1996), p. 24.

5   David Blankenhorn, *Fatherless America*, [New York: Harper Perennial, 1995], p. 10

6   United States Census Bureau, "Fatherless Children Statistics," National Fatherhood Initiative, www.fatherhood.org.

7   "Teen Suicide," Stanford Children's Health, www.stanfordchildrens.org.

8   David Blankenhorn, *Fatherless America*, [New York: Harper Perennial, 1995], p. 2.

9 Minnyvonne Burke, "Student Has Brain Damage after Bullying Incident Caught on Video, Lawsuit Says," August 14, 2019.

10 John Smithbaker on "James Dobson's Family Talk," interviewed by Dr. Tim Clinton, "Reaching and Healing the Fatherless," Aug 16, 2019.

Chapter Three: When a Son Closes the Door of His Heart

11 James Dobson, *Bringing Up Boys*, p. 36.
    Steve Hill, a former drug user turned evangelist, said, in his book *Time to Weep*, the concept that "real men don't cry" is a myth. He quoted Vice Presidential candidate Hubert Humphrey said, "A man without tears is a man without a heart" (William Frey II and Muriel Langseth, *Crying, The Mystery of Tears*, p. 99; cited in Stephen Hill, *Time to Weep*, [Orlando: Creation House, 1997], p. 61).

12 Gordon Dalbey, *Sons of the Father*, p. 221.

13 Ibid., pp. 29, 28.

14 If you find yourself exploding in anger, in an uncharacteristic way, this is a red flag. It warns you it's time to clean out all the unforgiveness that has been building through the years.

15 There are other causes such as abandonment by a mother or abuse by a relative.

16 Gordon Dalbey, Father and Son, n.p.

Chapter Four: Hanging from a Rope

17 Walt Mueller, "Teen Suicide..." March 7, 2019, CPYU.org.

18 Dr. Tim Clinton on James Dobson's "Family Talk," "Preventing Teen Suicide: Kids in Crisis," September 7, 2017.

19 Walt Mueller, "Teen Suicide..." March 7, 2019, CPYU.org.

20 James Dobson, *Bringing Up Boys*, p. 161; Amy M. Holmes, "Boys Today: Snakes, Snails and Guns," *USA Today*, 10 December 1999; cited in James C. Dobson, *Bringing Up Boys*, p. 34.

21 U. S. Department of Health/Census, "The Fatherless Generation," www.fatherlessgeneration.org.

Chapter Five: Angry Boys Shoot Bullets

22 Emilie Kao, "The Crisis of Fatherless Shooters," The Heritage Foundation, March 14, 2018.

23 Adding to the bitterness of a father-wound, when one's own father is cruel or absent, a son tends to see God as cruel or non-existent. Christian Psychologist Paul Vitz, in a message entitled "The Psychological Roots of Atheism," declared that "when the father is not present, the child naturally concludes there is no God" (Paul Vitz, "The Psychological Roots of Atheism," tape series produced by Allies for Faith and Renewal Conference, 1988, P.O. Box 8229, Ann Arbor, MI).

24 Peter Langman quoted in Bradford Richardson, "Link Between Mass Shooters, Absent Fathers, Ignored by Anti-gun Activists," The Washington Times, March 27, 2018.

25 Emilie Kao, "The Crisis of Fatherless Shooters," The Heritage Foundation, March 14, 2018.

26 Suzanne Venker, "The Ignored Correlation Between Father-lessness and Mass Shooters," The Stream, March 3, 2018.

Nikolas Cruz (Parkland shooter in Florida) was found to be on many meds. The SSRI antidepressants have side effects which can include mania, violence and obsessive suicidal intentions. The effects are more severe in children and teens whose brains haven't fully developed (Suzanne Venker, "The Ignored Correlation Between Fatherlessness and Mass Shooters," The Stream, March 3, 2018). Cruz's adoptive parents had both died, and his birth mother was a heavy drug user.

27 Joe Ehrman, TEDTALKx, "What It Means to Be a Man."

28 Anthony Simms, Facebook post, June 17, 2012, Ashland, California; cited in Warren Farrell, Ph.D., TEDx Talk, Marin, "The Boy Crisis: A Sobering Look at the State of Our Boys," published October 19, 2015.

29 Alexis Kleinman, Huffington Post, "Porn Sites Get More Visitors Each Month Than Netflix, Amazon, and Twitter Combined," updated Dec. 6, 2017, http://huffingtonpost.com.

30 Justin Sherman, CBS News, "Their Sexuality Has Been Hijacked: How Porn is Affecting America's Kids," November 14, 2019.

31 James Dobson, *Bringing Up Boys*, p. 210.

Chapter Six: "Dad, Where Are You?"

32 This true story took place 20 minutes from our camp, and Joshua Kelly has been one of our students and leaders at our camp. You might ask, "Is it legal to hold a meeting like this in a public school?" It is perfectly legal because students in the Christian Club had invited Joshua to preach.

In fact, the Equal Access Act of 1984 forbids public schools from receiving federal funds if they deny students their First Amend-ment right to conduct meetings because of "religious, political, philosophical or other content of speech at such meetings." While all non-violent religions should be respected, students should be given the option whether or not to attend these meetings of faith and values.

As a reminder, the first amendment in the Bill of Rights of the U.S. Constitution says, "Congress shall make no law respecting the establishment of religion or prohibiting the *free exercise thereof.*"

33 Jack Healy, Manny Fernandez, and Alan Blinder, "On a Spring Texan Morning, a Sound Heard too Often at Schools Across America: Bang. Bang. Bang," *New York Times*, May 19, 2018, NYT.com, accessed on August 5, 2018.

34 CNN reported that in 2019 in America, 45 school shootings took place in 46 weeks of school. That's one school shooting per week! Elizabeth Wolfe and Christina Walker wrote, "From Georgia to California. At elementary, middle and high schools. On college and university campuses," these shootings have taken place (Elizabeth Wolf and Christina Walker, CNN, November 19, 2019, www.cnn.com , accessed on December 13, 2019).

35 *The Washington Post*, "More than 236,000 Students Have Experienced Gun Violence at School Since Columbine," www.washingtonpost.com, April 20, 2018; John Woodrow Cox, Steven Rich, Allyson Chiu, John Muyskens and Monica Ulmanu, updated December 3, 2019, accessed December 13, 2019.

36 The reason I am including my book, *Dad, Where Are You?* in this story is because I have seen it impact so many young people and millennials. In fact, a mother wrote and told me what happened when her son, who was on heavy drugs, read *Dad, Where Are You?* (formerly called *The Pierced Generation*). On the night her son read this book, she could hear him sobbing in his room

as he looked at Jesus, bleeding and dying on a cross, and gave his life back to Christ. Years later, she said, "He is still walking with God."

37 Sandy Davis Kirk, *Dad, Where Are You?* (Lillian, AL: Behold Ministries, 2019), pp. 1-2.

38 Ibid., p. 11.

39 "I Can Only Imagine," track # 1, *I Can Only Imagine: The Very Best of MercyMe, Deluxe*," Bart Millard, 2018.

40 Sandy D. Kirk, *Dad, Where Are You*, pp. 49-50.
    Scriptures on the cup: Job 6:4, 21:20; Isa. 51:17-22; Jer. 25:15-29, 49:12; Ezek. 23:32-34; Hab. 2:16; Rev. 14: 10, 16:1. Matt. 26:39-43; Mark 14:36; Luke 22: 42-44; John 18:11. Also see 11 references in Romans on God's wrath.

41 "I Can Only Imagine," *The Very Best of MercyMe, Deluxe*, Bart Millard, 2018.

PART II: THE FATHER'S DAY RETREAT

Chapter Seven: When a Father Faces His Own Father Wound

42 Dave Roever with Karen Crews Crump, *Nobody's Ever Cried for Me* (Fort Worth, TX: Roever Communications, 1002), pp. 70-75; cited in Sandy Davis Kirk, *Dad, Where Are You?*, pp. 5-6.

43 Dave Roever with Karen Crews Crump, *Nobody's Ever Cried for Me*, 70-75; cited in Sandy Davis Kirk, *Dad, Where Are You?*, pp. 5-6.

44 Sandy Davis Kirk, *Dad, Where Are You?* p. 6.

45 The main camp house was the former home of Evangelist Steve Hill. Starting on Father's Day, 1995, Steve, along with Pastor John Kilpatrick, had led one of the greatest revivals in American history.

46 Hundreds of thousands of people, from all over the world, came to the altar of the church to give their lives to Christ. For at least five years, over four million people came to the Brownsville Revival in Pensacola.

Chapter Eight: A Father and Son Retreat (no notes)

Chapter Nine: No More Blaming God (no notes)

Chapter Ten: Healing the Father Wound (no notes)

Chapter Eleven: The Courage to Say "I'm Sorry" (no notes)

Chapter Twelve: The Power of Telling Your Story (no notes)

Chapter Thirteen: Gazing into the Father's Cup

47 The Greek word for "drops of blood" is *thrombos*, which means thick, heavy clots of blood.

48 See Jesus' prayer in Matthew 26:39-43; Mark 14:36; Luke 22: 42-44; John 18:11.

49 Jonathan Edwards, *The Works of Jonathan Edwards*, "Christ's Agony" (Edinburgh: Banner of Truth Trust, 1995), p. 687. Endnotes 155.

50 It's not that now you will never sin, but if you are a true Christian, you now have the power *not* to sin—all because Jesus poured out His sin-cleansing blood and drank the Father's cup.

51 What then is in this cup? It is not simply the scourging, the piercing thorns, the rejection of His people, the weeping of His mother, the spear that will pierce all the way up to His heart, Revelation 14:10 defines the cup as "the wine of the wrath of God, which is mixed full strength in cup." Jeremiah 25:15 defines the cup as being filled with "the wine of My wrath.

52 God told Moses, "Do not eat any of it raw or boiled at all with water, but rather roasted with fire....but whatever is left of it until morning, you shall burn with fire" (Exodus 12:10-11). This was to show that Jesus, the Lamb of God, would be roasted over the fire of God's wrath.

(If you would like to know more about the Father's cup, order my book *The Father's Cup or Undone by a Revelation of the Lamb* from our website: www. behold-ministries.org, or Amazon.com).

53 Charlotte Elliot, author of "Just As I Am," 1849.

Chapter 14: Overflowing Hearts (no notes)

Chapter 15: Affirming and Blessing Your Son

54 John Eldredge, *Wild at Heart: Discovering the Secret of a Man's Soul* (Nashville: Thomas Nelson, 2010) p. 45.

55 Gordon Dalbey, *Healing the Masculine Soul*, p. 151.

56 Gordon Dalbey, *Father and Son*, p. 6.

57 John Eldredge, *Wild at Heart*, pp. 61-62.

58 In his book, *The Mask of Masculinity*, Lewis Howes describes the masks men wear: The Stoic Mask, The Athlete Mask, The Sexual Mask, the Aggressive Mask, the Material Mask, The Joker Mask, The Invincible Mask, The Know-It-All Mask, and the Alpha Mask (Lewis Howes, *The Masks of Masculinity*, Rodale e-book).

59 Gordon Dalbey, video series, Part 5.

60 William Bennett, on "James Dobson's Family Talk, August 14-15, 2019.

61 The feminist movement brought equal pay for women, and no longer could a man abuse his wife or girlfriend and get away with it. But to emasculate men and equate God-given masculinity with something dark and toxic and a "social accident" is, in my opinion, a corrupt concept."

62 John Eldredge, *Wild at Heart*, p. 8.

63 Gordon Dalbey, *Father and Son*, story of Burt Reynolds on Johnny Carson, p. 201.

Chapter 16: The Most Beautiful Sound in the World (no notes)

Epilogue: Reach Out Your Hand

64 My younger sister, Debbie, has gone on to be with the Lord, but I always want to honor her with the distinction of initiating our father's salvation.

65 Joe Ehrmann, TEDx TALK, "Be a Man," Baltimore, 2013.

Made in the USA
Columbia, SC
30 May 2020